MW00438344

Alex White

ISBN 978-1-909455-22-1 (Paperback)
ISBN 978-1-909455-23-8 (Epub ebook)

Cover design © 2019 Dived Up Publications.

Cataloguing-In-Publication Data A catalogue record for this book can be obtained from the British Library.

Ebook *Get Your Boots On* is also available as an ebook.

Published 2019 by
Dived Up Publications
Oxford, United Kingdom
www.DivedUp.com

Red squirrel
Sciurus vulgaris

Get Your Boots On

Alex White

The author of the Foreword

Chris Packham has led a remarkable life.
He has gained recognition as a naturalist,
television presenter, writer, photographer,
conservationist, campaigner and filmmaker.

Herring gull
Larus argentatus

Foreword

Chris Packham

I read many books, always have, and get many rewards from that reading. Knowledge, information and entertainment are common prizes, occasionally sadness or joy, but rarely the wonderful reassurance I got from reading this fabulous and important book. It's good, it's inspirational and, critically, it's heartening.

There is no doubt that fewer young people are drawn to an interest in natural history at this time. Obviously it's not their fault, they have hardly any access to the natural environment and little encouragement to engage with it. Whilst their innate curiosity remains intact it simply isn't allowed the opportunity to be exercised — children and young people don't meet nature. We lock them up in an over sanitised and ostensively safe world, free from dirt, 'germs' and the risk of any harm and/or offer them too little time outside.

It is a tragedy, and it is dangerous because whilst their lives are seriously impoverished the long term result will be a human race which knows and cares less for the wild world. Just at the time when that world needs such knowledge and passion more than ever. Thankfully some youngsters slip through the net and Alex is one of them.

I'm lucky, I get the opportunity to try and share my own passion and enthusiasm with an audience on television. But relatively few of that audience are teenagers, and quite honestly, would teenagers really want to listen to me anyway? Maybe, a few, but I remember with cruel clarity that as a teenager myself, whilst I had an ear for aged experience, I also admired the energy and brutal ambition of youth. I listened to older people, learned from them, but was inspired by the determination and boldness of 'kids of my age'. That's why I think this book is important: it's written by a teenager for teenagers and therefore it can be wholly trusted by them.

And it exudes passion from every page, every idea, every encounter. The very fact it has been written and published is testament to the tremendous energy and determination that Alex musters. As such it's truly inspirational, both for the young and older reader. It covers a broad range of topics in a clear and concise way and provides you with a comprehensive toolkit which should instigate and encourage a keener interest in nature. It's both a manual and a guide, all illustrated with Alex's own photographs and filled with tips to make the fledgling naturalist's life easier.

There is only one bit I'd like to expand upon — activism. And I'll be frank. We are in trouble, big trouble. The adults have unfortunately elected idiocrasies to govern them, people who neither understand nor care for the dangerous predicament the planet is in. And they are not listening, not to their advisors, or the scientists or the people who know better. We don't have time to moan about this, we have to change things ourselves and that means standing up to be counted, it means shouting above the noise, it means taking action. Let me be very clear — I'm talking about peaceful, democratic action, using imaginative means. It might mean signing petitions, or marching, or simply sitting down in the street. And young people should be playing a central role in this. Not enough are yet, more need to wake up and realise that we've, I've, messed things up and that tomorrow's world is going to be their problem. So whether it's animal welfare, conservation or environmental protection it's very important that teenagers get aware and get active.

And this brings us back to the book, because to motivate such action a fuel is required, a boundless source of inspiration, a spark to light a fire that burns for a lifetime, an energy, a love. And as Alex, myself and all his contributors know there is none finer than connecting with nature. So read on, get up, get your boots on, get out and connect. There's no doubt that wildlife needs you, but we think you need wildlife too.

Chris Packham
New Forest, 2018

Fox
Vulpes vulpes

Contents

About the author

Alex White is a wildlife photographer and blogger. Since the age of ten, he has won a number of photography competitions. He has appeared on wildlife panels and spoken to audiences about his love of wildlife, from small local gatherings to BBC TV's *Springwatch Unsprung*.

Alex is passionate about British wildlife — in particular mammals — and keen to show other people how easy it is to find amazing wildlife on their doorstep. He continues to write his Appleton Wildlife Diary blog as a way to engage people with what goes on around his local patch in Oxfordshire.

Unless otherwise stated all wildlife photographs in this book which don't have Alex in them are his own work.

Roe deer
Capreolus capreolus

Fox
Vulpes vulpes

Water vole
Arvicola terrestris

To my family, both human and wild

I was born in July 1970 — a year after the moon landings. Those first grainy black and white images of Earth that were broadcast to the world, made us all start to realise the beauty and fragility of this planet we call home. When I was born the population of planet Earth was 2.3 billion. As I write it now exceeds 7 billion people.

By the time Alex reaches my age 9.5 billion people will inhabit this planet, putting an unsustainable burden on Earth's resources, which not only threatens the future of wildlife but the very basis of human civilisation.

The next 50 years could well be the most challenging period in the history of the human race. As Gihandi once said 'Man has enough for his needs but not his greed'.

To chart a path forward we need a new generation of passionate, inspiring and dedicated campaigners to protect our precious wildlife at home and abroad.

In Britain today Alex is prominent as a standard-bearer for this new generation of wildlife champions. Through his photography, writing and campaigning he is giving hope and inspiration to young people across this nation that despite all the challenges we face, it is still possible to make this world a better place for humans and wildlife.

Dominic Dyer — CEO of the Badger Trust & British Wildlife Advocate for the Born Free Foundation

1
INTRODUCTION

So what's this about?

I don't want this to be the type of book that your parents buy you for Christmas, which then gets looked through once and by the time you've written the 'Thank You' cards it's been shoved to the back of a shelf only to be rediscovered when you leave home.

I want this to be a well-thumbed-through, creased, dog-eared guide lounging at the bottom of a rucksack. A scribbled on, muddy, pages-faded book, lying under your bed amongst empty tea mugs and breakfast bowls filled with congealed cereal. Something you can open at any page, read backwards, from middle to beginning.

This book is for teenagers (or teenagers at heart), who have left behind their primary school years of jumping in puddles, running for the sake of running and not being afraid of who is judging them. It is for those who are now pressurised by schoolwork, mates, teachers, parents, exams, appearance, girlfriends/boyfriends and all the hassles that come with growing up.

In this book you will find

- How to start discovering the hidden world of wildlife;
- Where to go;
- Connecting to other teenagers with similar interests;
- Cool gadgets and technology (start writing that Christmas list now…);
- How to be an activist and stand up for what you believe in (basically how to get up people's noses and do what we teenagers do best); and finally
- Why we need to show those adults that we are the next generation and we actually want a planet decent enough to live on!

European badger
Meles meles

What's stopping you?

Plenty of things and lots of excuses. Being a teenager is incredibly difficult, your parents may say they understand — after all they were teenagers once — but they didn't grow up in a world full of technology.

Why should I go out when I can group chat with all my mates, have a laugh from the comfort of my own bedroom? Why should I go out looking at nature when I can play in a virtual reality world from a comfy chair and learn about the natural world from YouTube?

**Mysophobia =
Fear of germs,
contamination
or dirt**

Some parents can be obsessed that if we go outside we will come to some sort of harm. Some of us might get into trouble if we rip our jeans. If we come home muddy we might get moaned at about how much they cost, or our chances of falling ill. Luckily my parents aren't like this, but if yours are then get them to read what Ben Garrod has to say…

I genuinely believe we are a generation of naturephobes... where we don't like getting our hands muddy or our feet wet. If we turn our backs to nature we risk never knowing the world in which we live. We need to follow those lucky few who are always muddy, scratched and exhausted from a day outdoors.

Dr Ben Garrod—Evolutionary biologist and TV presenter

PHOTO: NORWICH
SCIENCE FEST

Broad-bodied chaser (male)
Libellula depressa

Okay, so if it's not your parents, maybe it's the other kids at school. Peer pressure is BIG. With groups and cliques it might be hard to fit in. Don't let this stop you being interested in wildlife because in every school there will be loads of other kids interested in the same things as you. A fascination with wildlife has given me some amazing friends and some brilliant opportunities.

There has been loads of research about the benefits of spending time outside with nature. The good news is it can help improve your mental health, physical fitness, decrease blood pressure and be good for the immune system. But for us teenagers it's mostly about having time to escape, getting away from the pressure of constantly being on social media and available to chat with. We shouldn't be worrying about our appearance and the next selfie!

When I'm old and sitting in a chair in a care home I'm not going to remember that YouTube video or that battle I won on my game console. What will bring a smile to my face is the memory of the first time I saw a badger cub or the feeling of exhilaration that seeing a whale, free, in the wild gave me.

Go wild
Alex

Getting interested and

GETTING OUT

2

Common kingfisher
Alcedo atthis

How do young people become interested in nature and the environment and keep that passion for a lifetime?

W I

My passion for wildlife was sparked by a number of sources all merging together around primary school years. At first, it was my parents being interested in nature and taking me out walking with our dogs, or badger watching. I was always surrounded by wildlife and felt that it was a big part of my life. I remember running as fast as my four-year-old legs would go through flooded fields in my wellies, coming home soaked to the skin. But most of all I remember laughing — laughing a lot!

I was also lucky to have a teacher who got me interested, but unlucky to be diagnosed with a long-term illness and have to come to terms with it. Nature has helped a great deal by being a stress reliever. The TV programme *Halcyon River Diaries* was important too, showing the ups and downs of watching wildlife and the everyday stories of a family with a passion for animals. It doesn't matter what or who has sparked your interest — whether it's a TV programme or your family. It doesn't matter how long you spend outside, walking to school or hanging out at the park — the best thing is that *the more you look, the more you see*. This might sound obvious, but the more you learn about wildlife the easier it is to notice even the smallest change in something that you pass by every day.

The more I learn and the more I ask the questions *Why?* and *How?* the more I become connected to nature and the more I realise how interesting everything is, the more time I want to spend outside.

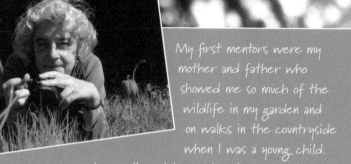

My first mentors were my mother and father who showed me so much of the wildlife in my garden and on walks in the countryside when I was a young child.

I was allowed to wander alone when I was eight, to my nearby local chalk stream with a glass jar held by a string handle, to fish for sticklebacks and watch water voles. In 1964, when I was eleven, watching wildlife was part and parcel of my life in my village. I used to wander across wildflower rich farm-land on my own at that age, as in those days all children did. Without mobile phones or cameras to hand, I had to rely on the joy of seeing a harvest mouse, kingfisher or an orange-tip butterfly as unforgettable, exciting memories that spurred me on to seek more wildlife.

If you have a passion for wildlife, my advice is to follow your heart, as it is one of life's most fulfilling interests which can make you feel as if you are walking on air when you have had an unexpected encounter with a pair of otters, or a hen harrier. If you are able to draw, photograph, give talks, write a book, or blog about wildlife, you can inspire children to take a closer look at nature. Just as Henry Williamson inspired me when I read *Tarka the Otter* at the age of 11. If you are a teacher, a Nature Table is another way of filling nursery and primary school children with awe and wonder, so that they are inspired to go out and explore the natural world. A special interest in wildlife often begins in childhood.

Jo Cartmell—Naturalist, photographer and blogger

Don't forget to take ...

Based on where you are going and how long for, the list of stuff to take could be endless. My essentials are always my camera and a decent pair of boots. Next is something to eat and drink. Even out on a short walk I seem to be forever peckish.

BLOG (May): Walking from my house down to the badger sett, the sun is setting. I am ready for a couple of hours of badger watching.

It is late spring, everything is growing — the ground underfoot is becoming greener and greener by the day. The scent in the air hangs heavy this time of evening.

My camera is under my coat, the trail camera ready to set up for the night and I've got pen and paper to make notes. I put my hands into my coat pockets, summer may be on the way but there is a chill to the air.

Anticipation is growing as I approach the edge of the wood. Will the badgers make an appearance? How many will there be? Will they come out of their sett before it is too dark

7-spot ladybird
Coccinella septempunctata

Depending on the weather and time of year a coat, hat or insect repellent may come in handy. One tip I picked up from listening to a wildlife photographer talk was to wear dark coloured gloves when taking photos so your fingers don't stand out against a black camera. You could actually fill a whole rucksack with stuff that *may* come in useful but you're the one who is going to have to carry it. Small items such as a notebook and spare SD cards and camera batteries can always be shoved in your pockets. Always check the camera before you leave the house as I've lost count of the times I've got into the field and realised my SD card is still in the side of the computer. Do I really need to mention about taking a phone, because who goes anywhere without one nowadays anyway?

Here's some excellent advice from Tom Moorhouse. He has spent many hours out in the field and is happy to share both his tips and mistakes.

I spent 14 years as a field ecologist in the UK. This means I had the most interesting, (mostly) stress-free and wonderful life of almost anyone I knew—one that was an absolute privilege. It also meant that: (a) I was very tanned—but only my arms and head; (b) I was incredibly fit (walking ten miles a day carrying field equipment for days, then weeks, then months is better than gym membership, trust me); (c) I got rained on more than anyone else I knew; (d) I got bitten by lots of interesting creatures; (e) I spent a lot of time in tents. So, here's my guide to personal field equipment...

Tom Moorhouse—Ecologist and author of The River Singers, The Rising, Adventures of Mr Toad and The Trickster.

1 **Britain can have four seasons in 24 hours.** I have spent summer days in the field with the weather switching every half an hour from 30 degrees and bright sunshine to ten degrees and pouring with rain ... then back again. For the whole day. I've been snowed on in April and cooked in October heat. You need to prepare for the extremes. So in the summer this means packing waterproof jacket, waterproof trousers and a fleece (rain can be COLD even in the summer). In the winter it means taking MANY layers of T-shirts and fleeces plus a waterproof jacket, gloves, hats and possibly thermal underwear.

2 **Waterproof trousers.** Yes, they look stupid. Yes, you probably need them anyway. Not only will they keep your legs dry but also channel the water down the outside of your boots. So they help your feet stay dry too. They can even act a bit like waders for a limited period of time, allowing you to cross shallow rivers that are deeper than your wellies.

3. **A note on waterproofs: expect them to die.** Hill walkers buy £300+ breathable jackets and trousers and know they are an investment. I have some posh jackets for days in hills and they are amazing. But if you're doing fieldwork in farms, woods, canals etc. they won't last a week. For fieldwork I bought a £50 ex-army jacket (cotton on the outside, water-proof inside) that's still going strong and a succession of £10 sacrificial waterproof trousers ready to be ripped to shreds on barbed wire.

4. **Wellies or walking boots.** This is your choice, depending on where you're going. Somewhere really wet with lots of puddles and streams is going to need wellington boots (and I've found that cheap wellies do as good a job as the expensive ones and can last longer). If you're mainly in the dry, go with walking boots.

5. **Shorts.** Don't do it. Wear trousers instead. In the field there are all sorts of bitey and pointy things that want to attack your lower legs. I wore shorts in the field only once. I spent that day walking through marshes and woods filled with knee-high nettles, razor-sharp sedges, brambles and midges. I vowed never to do it again.

6. **First aid kit and alcohol hand-gel.** All sorts of cuts and scrapes can be dealt with and disinfected in the field. The hand-gel is good when you need to eat lunch but suspect that the brown thing you just handled wasn't hygienic.

7. **A hat with a broad brim.** If you're somewhere with, um, enthusiastic insect life, it can confuse the horseflies and stops them from attacking your head. It also keeps rain out of your eyes / off your glasses, and stops you from getting heatstroke in the sun.

8   **Sun cream, factor 30 or higher.** Reapply it often, especially to the back of your neck and your ears. You will tan anyway, and it really isn't worth getting burned.

9   **Water.** Take LOTS (two litres at the very least on a hot day). It's heavy, but running out of water is horrible. Again, I did it once…

10 **Food.** Take LOTS. Cheese sandwiches are good because they don't spoil too badly if they get hot (meat that's been warm for a few hours can be a bit, um… yes). And lots of snacks. You're on your feet and walking, so you've earned those calories! My weapon of choice: Hobnobs (in a plastic bag).

11 **Mobile phone.** If it isn't a waterproof model, keep it in a zip lock plastic bag (or it will die in the rain). You need this for emergencies.

12 **Spare socks (in a plastic bag).** Because happiness is dry feet.

13 **For multiple days, a change of clothes for the evening.** (You probably won't carry this with you in the day) and deodorant (after a few days in the field you can't smell yourself any more — but others will).

14 **A day sack to put it all in.** Again, don't go expensive; it'll take a beating.

15 **An optimistic, can-do attitude.** Being outside is wonderful, but there will always be days when everything sucks. People appreciate someone who won't grumble when the rain is hammering, the wildlife is uncooperative, the map is turning to mush and water is running down his or her spine.

Stay safe

We've all heard the talk in school about staying safe and it's mostly all common sense:

Tell people where you are going and what time you'll be back. Not only so family know what time to expect you but to save the row when your dinner gets fed to the dog because you're an hour late home.

Take a phone. Preferably charged!

Go with a mate. Not only is this safer, but it's more fun. Four eyes are better than two when searching for animals.

Google Maps is great for planning in advance where you are going to go, but an **Ordnance Survey map** becomes helpful when you can't get a phone signal and has far more detail — especially when you get away from roads.

Stick to footpaths or get permission from the landowner before walking across fields.

Outdoors from indoors

Sometimes it amazes me how much wildlife I can see by just looking out of my window, not even putting a foot outside the front door.

Wren
Troglodytes troglodytes

The wren hopping around in the tree outside my bedroom, the cheeky rat stealing bird food in the back garden … the red kites calling, or the whoosh of geese wings overhead always draws me to look out of the window …

BLOG (July): From my kitchen door on a summer evening hedgehogs snuffle on the patio, entering the garden through a gap my mum cut in the fence. It must be an adult with two young. They drink some water from a small dish and very loudly crunch their way through the hedgehog biscuits I put out for them.

After eating their fill, they trot off in single file, edging along the bottom of the garden fence until they reach the gate where they squeeze through metalwork and off into next door's garden. **-- END**

Occasionally, I glimpse a wood mouse running from the bug hotel where it lives to the flowerbed and back, stealing seed that the pigeons have clumsily knocked off the bird table, pausing every few steps to listen out for danger.

If you don't have a garden or can't get outside, there are still ways to connect with wildlife:
- You could try planting a wildflower window box to encourage pollinating insects like bees, butterflies and some beetles;
- You can attract birds right up to your house by hanging feeders close to a window or using one that actually sticks to the glass.

Wildlife is always in need of water and will drink from practically anything — from an old saucer to a purpose-made birdbath.

Wood mouse
Apodemus sylvaticus

After being diagnosed with M.E.* at 17, I wanted to encourage others to connect with nature even if, like me, they can't always get outside. With BBC *Springwatch* I helped launch an online campaign #WildlifeFromMyWindow—a community space on social media to share sightings of nature from indoors. The hashtag receives thousands of photos and stories from people across the world who are housebound, in hospital, even indoors revising for exams, but who still enjoy seeing the beauty of nature each day. #WildlifeFromMyWindow is nature at its most accessible—for everyone.

Lizzie Guntrip—Writer, naturalist and campaigner

Lizzie's idea has been really popular and a great way of making wildlife-watching inclusive. For those with no way of getting outside or with an illness which prevents them, something as simple as connecting with wildlife can be a lifeline in a time of need.

Juvenile robin
Erithacus rubecula

* Myalgic Encephalomyelitis (M.E.) is a long-term (chronic), fluctuating, neurological condition that causes symptoms affecting many body systems, more commonly the nervous and immune systems. M.E. affects an estimated 250,000 people in the UK, and around 17 million people worldwide.

Garden

Your back garden is going to be the easiest and best place to watch wildlife. It is typical for people to overlook what goes on close to home, but there is something to see in even the smallest of back gardens.

My garden is where I can witness everything that goes on in a TV soap opera, from murder to love affairs, from family life to day-to-day survival and all just a few steps away from the kettle and fridge.

It's not just the obvious things like a sparrowhawk predating a tiny garden bird or a pigeon bringing up its family hidden deep inside the conifer tree. Looking closer, down on my hands and knees I can find multitudes of mini-beasts. On a summer's day, I can see armies of ants taking to the skies in search of a new colony or a battle to the death between a hornet and a wasp, little different from anything found in the latest video game.

Green woodpecker
Picus viridis

Most of these events go on daily, unnoticed, but our back gardens are very important places, especially in urban areas where they create safe havens and corridors from one wild area to another.

Eurasian sparrowhawk
Accipiter nisus **(juvenile)**

There are lots of ideas out there to encourage wildlife to your garden. Here is a selection of things you can try:

- Big ideas such as ponds and wild areas;
- Craft and building ideas such as compost heaps and bug hotels;
- A small hole in the fence for a hedgehog;
- Filling up the bird feeders or leaving out a tray of water — this will be gratefully received by both feathered and mammal visitors to the garden.

Using a trail camera is a great way to capture footage of the secret life of your garden. You will be amazed at what goes on!

PHOTO: KATE MACRAE

Kate MacRae in front of a trail camera

My garden is the place I use to practise my camera skills. I can spend time taking the same shot over and over again on different settings to find out what works best. Then I can nip back to the computer to check how the photos are turning out, before going out for a second attempt. That way when something spectacular happens I will hopefully be ready for it.

Fairly local

I think of my local patch as the places I can walk to. Secluded corners I can escape to after school or at the weekends.

The woods behind my house act like a sanctuary—a place to hide in, to badger watch, to catch up with characters that I'm acquainted with.

The fields nearby have well-trodden paths with familiar sights and sounds; the kestrel on the telephone line or the deers sat ruminating along the edges.

The river roaring as it passes through the weir with its multitude of swallows' nests precariously hanging only metres above the white water. Tiny nestlings' faces appearing amid the splashing water, waiting for their parents to return with food.

My school with its beech hedges full of chattering sparrows. The sports field with red kites, gulls and corvids which swoop down on left-over packed lunches as soon as the bell rings for the next lesson. Even waiting for the school bus each morning I can spend a few moments exchanging glances with a robin until the bus arrives and we go our separate ways.

All these familiar places I see day-in-day-out. I notice the changes, patterns that repeat themselves.

I see where the hares gather to box each spring; where the dragonflies hunt low over the meadow in the summer; where, in autumn, the redwings and fieldfares collect in large numbers to strip the hawthorn hedges of their berries and in turn the buzzards arrive to watch them and wait for their next meal. In winter I hear the calling of the tawny owls disputing their territories and the raven high on the pylon with its throaty 'kraa' call outlined against the metallic grey sky.

Your local patch is where you can seek out your wild-life neighbours and learn who it is you share your home range with.

Roe deer (female)
Capreolus capreolus

37

Further afield

Still classed as my local patch I think of 'further afield' as locations around the county I live in that I can get to within an hour or so, making a half or full-day outing. The problem is I also need someone to drive me there!

There are brilliant venues such as local Wildlife Trust areas, nature reserves, reservoirs and parks. You can search wildlifetrusts.org for details. RSPB Otmoor in Oxfordshire is one of my favourite places.*

BLOG (January): I come over to Otmoor every year to see the murmurations but it is a bit hit-or-miss as to whether the starlings put on a display or go straight down to roost. An afternoon's murmuration can start with one small group of birds twisting and turning at a very low level. Looking up into the distance I see the familiar shape of black clouds made up of hundreds of starlings. One to the east, one to the west, one south and one north. Starlings come in from all around. On arriving they quickly join in with the groups already present, making patterns in the sky that change as quickly as a blink of an eye.

Rather than the mind-blowing patterns in the sky, this particular evening the starlings poured down into the reed beds, wave after wave, like a mini tornado, which was no less impressive. Thousands-upon-thousands flowing down from the sky to the land. The beats of their wings making an undulating sound like waves on a beach. Their chattering growing louder and louder as more starlings descended.**--END**

---

* RSPB = Royal Society for the Protection of Birds.

There's nothing more exciting than having a passion. Nothing that lights up a person's soul more than having something they really care about. You might love earwigs, maybe you're mad about newts or perhaps you're fascinated with fungus. Whatever it is, NEVER LOSE THAT ENTHUSIASM and don't let anyone tell you that it's not cool. There is nothing cooler than a person who steps away from the masses and shapes their own path, even if that path takes them wading into muddy rivers every weekend and ends with them covered in pondweed.

Dr Jess French — Vet, zoologist, TV presenter and author

Due to the time involved, there are places I can normally only get to over the weekend or during school holidays when the rest of my family haven't got other plans. I'll probably only visit them once or twice a year unless something pops-up on social media — a report that a rare bird has been spotted, perhaps — then I have to be extra nice to my parents to have any chance of getting to see it.

It is well worth signing up for newsletters and looking out for special events and open days for such areas as nature reserves. These can make the travelling time and cost justifiable to your parents. Although if there are tons of people around you might not always get the best view, this is not a problem as you'll get to hang out and learn stuff anyway.

Kimmeridge Bay, Dorset

Being sensible around wildlife

It is very easy to get carried away, creeping closer and closer to get a better look or that perfect photograph of a particular animal or bird. But take a moment to think about how you are affecting that animal's behaviour.

Are you frightening it?

Are you stopping it from feeding its young?

Are you disturbing it?

Some animals and birds are protected by law, including common species. The main point is that you should not disturb them. This is especially important during breeding or nesting times. It is worth checking which ones you need a licence to take photos of. For more detail either search the Government website (www.gov.uk) for 'Protected species: when to apply for a licence to survey, film or photograph them', or Rare Bird Alert (rarebirdalert.co.uk) for 'Photographing schedule 1 birds'.

European otter
Lutra lutra

Fieldcraft

Wildlife is commonly shy and who can blame it? It has a lot to fear from human beings in general. Whether deliberately or by accident we can make life pretty difficult for other species. We can't really complain when animals run in the opposite direction as we approach! This is where fieldcraft comes into its own. Fieldcraft is the art of *travelling*, *hiding*, *finding* and *taking photos* undetected, or at least without scaring the wildlife into doing a disappearing act…

BLOG (June): The smallest badger cub shuffled closer and closer to me. I was holding my breath, wondering whether, if I took a photo, the click would scare it away. Slowly, it came so close I could have reached out and touched it. I was very aware that Arrow and the other cub were just behind and off to my left. I could hear two more cubs play fighting in the brambles. My legs were starting to go numb and I really wanted to move. I knew that if I moved even slightly Arrow might feel threatened, stamp her front paws, raise her head to make herself look bigger, all the while showing her teeth and grumbling.

As I was
lying down I
knew I wouldn't
be able to get out of
the way, so I stayed still
while, bit by bit the feeling
drained out of my legs.

The cub came so close we were
nose to nose. It looked straight into my
eyes and I looked into its. For a spilt second
it seemed as if I was one of them. The cub then
turned and trotted back under the brambles.**--END**

Signs

First thing is to actually track down the wildlife. Local knowledge and experience is needed (or at least being good with Google). There is no point in searching for red squirrels in your area if they aren't there to be found.

Once you are in the right area, look for signs. Each creature leaves its own calling mark. Footprints and tracks, scats and latrines, homes or nests and feeding activity. Some can be quite clear, other signs will become more obvious with experience, like badger snuffle holes or hare forms.

Keep still or move slowly

Many animals will scarper when they see you. When I first come across something I want to take a picture of I always take the first photo — 'get one in the bag' — then creep a little closer. This could be standing up or on hands and knees. Then I take another photo, creep a little closer, and take another. You get the gist. I'm now where I want to be without disturbing the animal.

Many wildlife photographers use hides or camouflaged clothing. This can be really useful if you are watching the same area or same animals over a longer period of time. But with nowhere to hide or disguise yourself the art of learning to creep closer and closer unseen or without disturbing wild animals involves real skill.

Be quiet

Anything from heavy steps to a rustling coat, talking to your mates or a camera shutter click can be heard by wild animals. Overall they have much better hearing than we do.

Red fox
Vulpes vulpes

Smell

The 'Lynx effect' doesn't work on wildlife. Smelling of products, takeaways or fabric softener will have a badger or other wildlife sniffing you out from a mile away. The chances of seeing anything except birds will be zero (most birds have no sense of smell). So, check the wind direction and stand downwind.

— — — — — — — — — — — — —

BLOG (May): There it is, the smell of fox. If you know it, I don't have to describe it, it is unmistakable.

As I walk down the field, it is early evening, the heat is still heavy on the ground, as I pass gaps in the hedge the temperature changes, dipping then rising. The smell of elderflower drifts up my nose, another couple of steps and it has gone.

I settle down on the ground with my back against the largest oak tree, this gives at least some cover to stop the wind blowing my scent everywhere. I now can't smell anything but the warm dry earth. I sit awhile, waiting, watching.

There it is again, that musky, fruity, sharp smell that can only be a fox. I can't see it but I know somewhere behind the brambles it is patiently watching me.

I have done as much as I can to cover my scent, I'm downwind, I have my hood up, my coat is the one I never wash but leave in the porch. I expect this fox smelled me metres away. Certainly if I can smell the fox, it can smell me.

As the sharp musky smell (which for some reason reminds me of liquorice) fades, I presume the fox has sneaked off undetected and taken the long way round.**--END**

— — — — — — — —

The hardest thing as a teenager is wanting to fit in. You are always thinking about what your peers are thinking of you, and this has such an impact on our dreams at that time. I know, I experienced it first hand and it made me question everything I did. Now, much older (not necessarily wiser) I really regret not following my dreams at that time…who knows, maybe if I had, I'd be as famous as Ray Mears!!!

Once I got over what others were thinking about me and with the guidance of an amazing geography teacher, I fell in love with the natural world. It brought out my curiosity in everything around me. I wanted to know everything about everything!

The most important and hardest thing I learnt (and am still learning) is how to move in and observe nature. Nature works at its own pace and we have to learn to move with it and not against it. You have to put yourself in the mind of the animals you want to see. Many animals will allow you to approach them if you are relaxed, move calmly, slowly and take your time.

There are two approaches if you want to get close to nature. First, conceal yourself so the animal does not know you are there. Drab natural coloured clothing that blends in with your environment will help here. Remember to cover your face and hands.

Secondly, stalking. This takes time and lots of skill and patience to perfect. To be good at stalking, you need a good understanding of your quarry—how to recognise signs of its presence, when to see it, how to track it and, most importantly of all, how to get close enough without it disappearing.

Also consider other wildlife, particularly birds as they are the first to raise the alarm and let all the other animals know that you are near. Observe wind direction, ideally it should be blowing toward you, this will help blow your smell away from what you are stalking (and forget the deodorant!).

So how do you get good at fieldcraft I hear you ask? Simple really—get out there and practise, practise and practise some more.

Manse Ahmad—Bushcraft and Primitive Skills Instructor, Wilderness Pioneers

Adder *Vipera berus*

Traces

You can look for tracks in mud, sand or snow. The muddy track was made by a badger. The snow print was made by a rabbit. Keep an eye out for other signs of wildlife, like this rabbit fur left after a predation, or feathers, nests and discarded nut shells. If you are lucky enough you may come across a buzzard plucking post.

PHOTO: DAN BOLT

Grey seal
Halichoerus grypus

Adventurous wildlife

This is the stuff of legends. The kayaking, the scuba diving, the likes of Steve Backshall and Andy Torbet. Whether you are looking for animals that are underwater, on the water, up a tree or in other hard-to-reach places, training, safety and a sense of adventure is important.

Activities such as rock climbing, coasteering, mountaineering and free-diving all need proper training and experience. But snorkelling, mountain biking and hiking can all be done with a small amount of training, local knowledge and a fair amount of common sense. They will enable you to get to see animals that choose to live in out-of-the-way or awkward places such as cliff faces:

- **Snorkel** to see impressive marine animals like basking sharks, seals and jellyfish close-up;
- **Cycle** at places such as RSPB Rainham Marshes. You can rent bikes (or take your own) and follow a trail, taking in butterflies and dragonflies,

Basking shark
Cetorhinus maximus

passing waders, sea birds and resting seals. Plenty of areas such as the Yorkshire Dales and the Brecon Beacons have designated paths so you won't disturb the wildlife, especially ground nesting birds. Imagine cycling along with the wind on your face and ospreys overhead;

- **Hike** along the South West Coastal Path the UK's longest National Trail and spot birds like peregrines, guillemots and maybe even marine mammals like dolphins. Find hidden waterfalls in Wales, or moss and lichen covered trees and boulders in Wistman's Wood, Devon;

- **Don't forget** the importance of local knowledge from tourist information centres, especially regarding the effect that the weather and tides might have.

Peregrine falcon
Falco peregrinus

There are so many fun activities which will also get you close to nature, for example:

- Gently **kayaking** up the river and floating right under a kingfisher;
- **Surface diving** under the water with a playful seal;
- Looking for **glow-worms** late at night;
- On the coast you can climb over seaweed-covered rocks while **coasteering**, or look for crabs and tiny fish in rock pools at low tide. Then you can even build a fire on the beach and toast marshmallows while the sun goes down;
- If you are feeling really adventurous you can discover bats, stalagmites and stalactites in **underground caves and passages**.

These activities are best done in groups with a trained instructor, so all the more reason to get your mates to join in.

PHOTO: VIV CUMMING

It's harder to find a freer feeling than the rush of endorphins and a load of salty water up your nose after a close underwater encounter with a sea lion. Or running in the snowy Brecon Beacons with icy wind blowing into your face as you squint up watching a red kite circling above you. Some of my most treasured moments with wildlife are those where I am up against the elements. I have always loved getting my 'hands dirty' when it comes to understanding more about an animal by experiencing their habitat, sensing what they do and intently observing their behaviours. I believe deep down we all have this connection with nature but our generation have become a little less curious as we live through the screens on our phones. While I have been very lucky to have encounters with extreme wildlife all over the world, actually you don't need to venture to the ends of the Earth to experience this. So, if I could give any advice to those that seek adventure and wildlife encounters it would be to just get out there. Whether it's walking, sitting, camping, wild swimming—whatever—take the time to get out there and put yourself in unfamiliar surroundings. The sounds, smells, fleeting movements in the trees that catch your eye, why not venture off the beaten track and I guarantee it will surprise you! Some of my most memorable encounters with extreme wildlife are right on my doorstep. Watching a pair of the world's fastest birds the peregrine falcon hunting over Bristol city centre or watching complex social dynamics in cannibalistic larvae in the leaf litter beneath my feet. Now that is extreme!

Lizzie Daly—Wildlife biologist and presenter

Urban wildlife

Rolling green fields, woods and endless skies are what normally spring to mind when talking about wildlife-watching. However, many animals and birds either don't have any choice other than to share our cities with us or use our built-up areas to their advantage.

Rose-ringed parakeets in St James Park, London *Psittacula krameri*

From the foxes of Bristol to peregrines on city cathedrals. The thousands of starlings in Brighton to deer in London. Even the local supermarket car park hosts wildlife beauties if you bother to look closely. Places such as canal towpaths, railways sidings and churchyards often go undisturbed and can host a wide variety of animals and birds. Urban streets and car parks can be full of discarded food which wildlife is quick to take advantage of. Many successful photographers specialise in urban wildlife, with some stunning results.

BLOG (October): Sitting in the car in the rush hour traffic, vehicles all around belting out fumes, snippets of conversation, the latest tracks on the radio seep through the air. On the pavement two jackdaws fight over a dropped chip, unseen underfoot by most people rushing home from work and schools. Their heads down and phones to their ears, they fail to notice the brilliant blue of the jackdaws' eyes and the deep black gloss of the feathers as they hurry home in a world of their own.**--END**

**Common starlings
at the London Eye**
Sturnus vulgaris

Private gardens and
parks make up a network
of territories and pathways for
larger mammals such as badgers.
While you may see signs you may never
actually see the animals unless with some of
them you are walking home in the dark.

Humans and urban wildlife often come
into conflict with each other. This is hardly
surprising, after all, we are trying to do the same
things: have somewhere safe to live, find something to eat and go about our business. We share
the same space but animals don't obey our laws.

Iconic UK wildlife

Want to go even further or plan a week away? There are loads of iconic places to see amazing wildlife around the country. There are also lots of great guidebooks already available so I'm just going to mention a few places that I have experienced for myself.

RSPB Ham Wall, Somerset — Starlings

This is one of the best places to see starling murmurations. I'm not kidding, over one million starlings creating patterns in the sky. Arriving at lunchtime on a chilly February day gave our group the chance to look around Shapwick Heath Nature Reserve first. This reserve is in the Avalon Marshes which are full of mystical wildlife such as otters, bitterns, great white egrets and many other wetland-loving birds.

Once at Ham Wall, we didn't need any local knowledge about where to go to see the starlings — we just followed the crowds of people with cameras and tripods.

It can be a bit hit-and-miss, the starlings may come in from a different direction each night depending on the wind and weather, but there was time to move along slightly to get in a better position. There is nothing in the world to describe the sound of a million birds passing overhead and not even the best photograph can capture the bril-liance of the swirls and shapes, not to mention the raining poo!

— — — —
BLOG (February):
As the darkness slowly began to fall, small groups of starlings started to fly over our heads, shortly followed by groups of ever increasing numbers. As the flocks of birds got bigger, so did the noise. One group seemed never ending, as a long path of starlings flew overhead. As more and more starlings arrived, the murmuration started to form. Its twists and turns moving from left to right and back again. The tiny black dots jostling for space within the huge entity that made nature's patterns in the sky.--**END**
— — — —

Lundy Island, Devon (Bristol Channel) — Seals

Lundy Island off the north coast of Devon has a colony of seals that is used to being visited by divers and snorkellers. Skippers of local boats willingly inform visitors of the dos and don'ts of getting into the water with the seals. Tips include: not to look them straight in the eye, not to approach them, to let them freely come to you.

It is one of the best feelings in the world (and a bit nerve racking) to have a wild seal come up and want to play with you. They are just like a marine version of a large, unruly puppy. A GoPro or underwater camera is a must.

Cardigan Bay, Wales — Dolphins

On the west coast of Wales, New Quay harbour wall is a fantastic place to watch dolphins play without having to leave dry land.

Timing the tides right and arriving just before high water* on a summer's day, you can grab a bag of chips, settle down with some bins or a camera and listen to the oo's and ahh's (just like at a firework display) of the lines of people watching dolphins jumping, diving, twisting and turning a few hundred metres from the shore.

Bins = A pair of binoculars

Dolphin by Charlotte O'Neill, illustrator and artist

* Check the local tide times before travelling!

Skomer Island, Pembrokeshire, Wales — Puffins

Not the easiest reserve to get to, the Wildlife Trust only lets a certain number of people onto the island per day, so it's an early start to get in the queue for the boat across. Once on Skomer, head towards The Wick where you can watch puffins coming in to land or flying over the cliff edges.

At certain times of year the footpaths are covered with puffins and the clumsy little birds are every-where — pushing and shoving each other as they pop up their heads out of their burrows (they nest under-ground). When we visited there were around 50 puffins spread along the cliff, plus hundreds more in the water, in the air or waddling along the paths.

Skomer is also a great place to spot dolphins, seals, peregrines and guil-lemots. The best time for puffins is between April and the end of July.

BLOG (May): The path carved out over time by thousands of footsteps holds more people sat with cameras than puffins. The puffins stand just off the path in groups of two or three looking like they are discussing what these humans are all about that arrive each day by boat.

I'm not sure whether to aim my camera to the sky to catch a puffin in flight as it comes in to land, or watch out for their comical heads appearing randomly out of the ground.

Their bright colourful beaks contrast against the grey sky so I decide to go for a photo of one as it flies in over the water.--**END**

Puffin
Fratercula arctica

WHAT TO SEE

January
- The bare branches suddenly become luminous yellow with hazel catkins;
- Listen in the night for the eerie sound of mating foxes;
- Look out for the spectacular sight of a starling murmuration — thousands of birds taking to the air, making mesmerising patterns in the sky.

February
- Great crested grebes begin their amazing courtship ritual;
- A great time to watch short eared owls hunting during the day;
- Watch red squirrels chasing each other up trees as the mating season begins.

March
- Boxing hares are one of the signs of spring. The 'boxing' is normally a female fending off an over-amorous male;
- Get up early and listen to the dawn chorus. Birds are attracting a mate, calling other members of their flock or defending a breeding territory;
- Millions of coastal birds migrate from the sea to their breeding colonies.

April
- Hedgehogs start being more active. If you cut a small hole in your garden fence you may even get one visiting you;
- Solitary bees start emerging after winter;
- Listen out for the first cuckoo calling as these birds return to the UK.

May
- Ancient woodland will be covered with a carpet of bluebells;
- Basking sharks appear along our coastline. Best sightings are in the south west of England, the Isle of Man and the west coast of Scotland;
- The first swallows will start arriving back from Africa. Listen out for their distinctive twitters, chirps and warbling overhead.

June
- Watch bats flitting about the night sky after flying insects;
- Calm and sunny days are best for spotting some of the UK's 59 different species of butterflies;
- Find a local badger-watching group and see cubs venture out of their sett for the first time.

July
- Between 10 pm and midnight female glow-worms emit a bioluminescent light to attract mates;
- Best time to get some great views of adult puffins flying back and forth from the sea to nest with food for their chicks;
- Ladybird season is in full swing. There are 46 species in the UK to look for, although only 26 are the classic ladybird round shape with spots.

AND WHEN

August

- Lazy summer days are just perfect for exploring rock pools. Look out for crabs, anemones, shrimps, small fish and even starfish;
- The sound of grasshoppers and crickets on a summer's evening and through into the night is a definite sign the summer is in full swing;
- Hunting backwards and forwards across meadows and near rivers dragonflies and damselflies are great to watch.

September

- Thousands of geese and swans, such as whooper and Bewick's swans, Brent, barnacle and pink footed geese, make a breathtaking sight passing over head as they arrive back in the UK;
- Morning mist begins to hang in the fields as the nights start to get colder. Look out for spider webs covered in dew;
- September is the beginning of seal season around the coastal areas of Wales, with some 3,000 pups being born. In Scotland the season can be in October, and even November to December in Lincolnshire.

October

- In parks and fields all over the UK, rival male deer will be fighting for their right to mate. Red deer, fallow and sika will be rutting. Early morning is their most active time;
- There are over 15,000 different types of fungi found in the UK, now is the best time to search for them in woodlands, parks and gardens;
- Autumn colours — in woodlands all over the country trees have changed from the green of summer to picturesque patterns of gold, red, orange and yellow.

November

- Many creatures are making the most of the last moments before the winter really sets in. Watch out for insects feeding on ivy flowers, or rooks gathering in large groups;
- Clear skies mean November is great for stargazing. You'll need to find a place where light pollution isn't too bad;
- The combination of winter storms, rough seas and high tides can produce the best chance of finding fossils on beaches.

December

- December might not be an obvious time for bird-watching, but with no leaves to obscure the view birds are easier to spot. Many, such as the winter migrant thrushes, fly around in large flocks;
- Mountain hares in their white winter coats can be seen in Scotland and the Peak District;
- Snow and ice make for fantastic photo opportunities, whether wide-angle landscapes or close-up (macro) photography.

Mya, Alex, Arjun, James, Alex, Kabir, Aryan

Making
CONNECTIONS

3

Don't panic, but being interested in wildlife can make you seem a bit of a loner. So, no problem if that's your thing. But spending hours out in a field or alone in some woods getting to know the animals can sometimes come at the expense of human connections.

By its nature, wildlife-watching tends to be a solitary hobby. But there are likely to be hundreds of other young adults in your area who have the same interests. If you want to, you just need to connect with them. Spending the day out with your mates is fun and the feeling amongst the group when someone spots something exciting or bags a great photo is unbeatable.

— — — — —

BLOG (July): It's mid after-noon in a village garden. On the patio, the table is laid for ten. Food is piled high and everyone is enjoying chatting about the wildlife walk we have just taken.

The red kites soaring overhead, the hares peeping out from the maize field and the couple of roe deer passing the time, are all part of the conversation as food is passed around the table.

The topic changes to what was going to take place after the meal. Plans are made, talks about which camera to take, would jumpers be needed? Who was going to stand where — we were preparing to go badger watching.**--END**

— — —

The sharing of information, stories and photos at the end of a day of wildlife watching is a friendship goal. Turning up at a hide and seeing familiar faces, exchanging and comparing notes and catching up makes you feel part of a group. Once you have made these connections with other wildlife enthusiasts they will remain for a very long time.

Common blue
Polyommatus icarus

I loved butterflies as a teenager and I was terrified of being exposed as a nerd. I never told any friends about my passion. I wish I had shared it because many of my friends have grown up to love nature too.

Today I would tell my 15-year-old self—and any other teenagers—to seek out like-minded people on social media and be proud of who you are. Be as public or as private about your passion as you want to be but never let anyone make you feel inferior—an appreciation of creatures other than ourselves is the most attractive and important quality we can possess.

Patrick Barkham—Author and fan of butterflies, badgers and all wildlife!

65

Spread the word

We spend our days connecting with hundreds of people. Using any type of social media is an awesome way of finding out what is going on and hooking up with other wildlife enthusiasts. Whether it is forums, Twitter, Facebook or Instagram, communicating through social media can help you find local groups, upcoming events, competitions and advice on the best places to spot animals. It encourages you to share information, ask lots of questions and get outside and seek out more wildlife.

There will always be someone out there who knows the answers to your questions. Most people are friendly, encouraging and happy to help, for example, identifying a species. Or you can stay in the background picking up tips and information by reading what people are up to.

The great thing about social media is that it crosses boundaries. You could be talking to a famous person one minute and a mate down the street the next. One of my coolest instances was when I found out someone I had been chatting to for a while actually went to the same school as I did. Without social media I never would have known that they were into wildlife as much as me.

YouTube is excellent for getting hints and tips about photography and forums are great for talking about environmental and animal welfare issues. Finally, take a look at a few e-magazines as there are now some great ones aimed at young people, e.g. check out *New Nature — The Youth Nature Magazine*.

PHOTO: ROBERT VIVANCOS

Social media is a great way to connect with people and learn about the natural world. Linking up with specialist groups on Facebook and following naturalists on Twitter keeps me up-to-date and always turns up something new and incredible. It can be a real laugh too, you never know what conversation you'll end up having and it's an easy way to keep in touch with connections all over the globe.

Bonnie Griffin — Natural history curator

Being wise online

Social media is fun as long as you stick to three rules:

Responsibility: I came across this phrase which I really like: 'positive digital footprint'. Anything you put out on social media is (potentially) there forever. So, while something may seem funny at the time, think about whether you would want your future employer, your parents or your teachers seeing it! Will it be cringe-worthy in a few days, weeks, months or even years' time?

Risk: Simple really. Don't give out personal information, don't meet anyone alone and don't tell anyone where you are going to be, always report retrospectively.

Respect: If you have nothing positive to say, then don't say anything.

Blogging

A blog is basically an online diary. It can be long or short, loads of details or just a few lines jotted down. There are plenty of platforms to choose from depending on whether you want just the rolling blog or extra pages to showcase who you are and what you are about. There are tons of people out there who have become famous and run businesses from blogging.

I love looking back over mine and reminding myself of places I have visited, people I have met and the animals I have spent time with. One of my most poignant blogs was when 'Cookie', a badger that I had been following for two years, got hit by a car. She had been lactating and my family and I spent a few weeks looking for her orphaned cubs. I had comments and messages from all over the world from people who had followed Cookie's adventures on my blog. Don't worry it had a happy ending...

BLOG (April): Cookie is one of the badgers from my local sett. She was born in 2014 when the sett had ten badgers in it. She was one of three cubs that year. She is very distinctive because she has part of her ear missing. Cookie also has a diamond shaped tail, which is thin next to her rump then is very bushy.

I have followed her over the past two years. Watching her grow, eat, play, interact with the rest of the badgers and collect bedding. She also is very good at finding my trail camera and sticking her face up to the lens. She even came up to our house sometimes. During this time the number of badgers in the sett went down to six or seven.

The sett is on private land, which we are very lucky enough to have written permission from the landowner to watch the badgers. On Tuesday evening I went down and watched Cookie and two other badgers, including Pirate (the badger with only one eye) who we think is Cookie's littermate. I took this photo just after 8 pm. Cookie is the badger at the back.

At 9.33 pm she appeared on the trail camera for the last time. At 6.30 am my dad found a badger dead on the road a few hundred metres from our house. Mum went up to check and confirmed it was Cookie and that a car had hit her.

Unfortunately, Mum also noticed that Cookie had been lactating, so there were cubs somewhere. Although all the hair on her stomach had been worn away where she had been feeding, her teats looked like they were dry, so we hoped that she had the cubs as early as December and had been weaning them.

I cannot explain how upset I was when I heard about Cookie. My feelings went from sadness to anger. I felt heartbroken. I know Cookie was a wild animal and as someone who wants to photograph wild animals as a career I shouldn't get involved, but it is very difficult not to. It made me feel like I didn't want to carry on taking photos or blogging.

I have been overwhelmed by the amount of support on social media I have had over Cookie. I didn't realise how many people followed what she got up to. We took advice from lots of people about what to do about the cubs, but it was just a case of monitoring the sett day and night.

On Wednesday night it was really hard to watch the badgers. Mum and I stood at the edge of the sett and cried. We kept thinking we would see her and mum had made a mistake in identifying her. Pirate was around and so was a male.

Mum checked the sett a few times during the day while I was at school. On Thursday night, three badgers snuffled around the sett before heading off into the fields.

Last night Jo came around to try and help us find the cubs. Jo and I stayed by the sett, while mum went off to check some of the outlying setts. In the first five minutes Pirate came out, then another two, both of which I recognised. Then finally what we think is a cub came out. I tried not to get really excited. This badger is about a third of the size of the others, its face much thinner, not the triangular shape of the adults, and with a stubby nose. The middle strip on its face is whiter and fluffier than the adults. Finally, its whole coat is fluffier and almost shiny. It was getting too dark to take any good photos.

I am slightly cautious about saying this is Cookie's cub because it was much bigger than the cubs were this time last year. They were this size by 15th June. It seemed to be coping very well on its own. It hung around with the others but not as close to them as last year's cubs were with their mum. It didn't go very far away from one of the entrance holes. I am really hoping that this is Cookie's cub, and I am going to carry on monitoring the sett for the next few weeks. Sleep tight, Cookie.--**END**

A couple of weeks later we found six cubs, four with another adult female and two more which we think were Cookie's. In the end five cubs survived.

Entrance to a badger sett

Local groups

Scary! This is the real world. No seriously, it is all very well chatting away online, but joining a local group is one of the best ways to get out and learn more about your local patch.

I've had good and bad experiences with local groups. Some don't seem that welcoming to younger people and it can be quite intimidating turning up when everybody already knows each other and you are the only young person there. But you have to persevere and find the right one for you.

BLOG (April): Nervously standing in the car park amongst a group of volunteers waiting to help out with a small mammal survey. The volunteers ranged from an excited seven-year-old through to university students to ecologists with some serious knowledge.**--END**

The organiser was trying to split us into groups to enable us to all have the best experience from the day. I stood on the edge, half hoping that I wasn't going to be treated like a primary school kid, but also worried about being shown up for lack of knowledge and experience. My fears were unfounded. Although I was the only person in my group not studying or already qualified for a degree in ecology or zoology everybody treated me as an equal.

I now belong to a number of awesome local groups that are encouraging, and keen to teach young adults and younger kids alongside everyone else. There have been opportunities to help out on stalls, go on training courses, attend talks, volunteer and assist with citizen science projects. Ask around, find out what your local groups can offer you. At the end of the day it's people like us who will be running these groups in years to come.

Every school is different and I think a lot depends on your teachers' interests and enthusiasm. Primary school tends to have much more involvement with nature, with their forest schools, nature tables and projects, as well as trips outside the classroom. These seem to melt away once secondary school starts.

When you first start at secondary school you just want to fit in and make friends. Everybody forms gangs, groups or squads. Within these there is a hierarchy. Some want to be the tough one, some the leader, some the popular one, others just want to be a part of it all. Having wildlife as a hobby can sometimes be deemed as being uncool, weak, caring. You can be abandoned or excluded from some of the groups.

Don't stress, be true to yourself and stick with your interests. If your school doesn't already have a wildlife or environmental club then form your own group, set up your own lunchtime club. This might seem difficult to do — it can be against the culture in secondary school — but you won't get anywhere without trying. Get in contact with organisations such as the Wildlife Trust who will help you. There will be other kids that will be really grateful you did.

I was lucky enough to live in the countryside where I could hop over the fence and go for a walk on my own or jump on my bike and visit local birding spots. But I was also very lucky that my school had a good natural history club. I had school friends who shared my interest. That experience was impor- tant in establishing my interest in birding and many of the friends from those days are friends still — and birding still.

Dr Mark Avery — Author

It is very hard to be different to people around you. I remember it clearly myself, and I saw what happened to people who didn't follow the crowd. I can see those pressures in my two sons too. And it is too easy for older people to say—'just be yourself and don't worry about what others think'. I would have found that really difficult. A while ago, someone gave me a very good piece of advice. It's easy to follow and surprisingly powerful. Carry around a very small stone in your pocket. Mine is white and smooth and about the same size as a peanut M&M. I found it on a beach. Remember, he said, that stone is what is really you inside, the bit of you that is unique and independent of the rest of the world. Whenever you feel lost or worried or unsure, slip your hand into your pocket and hold the stone. It is comforting and empowering to hold onto when you feel challenged. That stone can represent your love of the natural world. Hold onto it.

Even if, at the moment, you can't be too open about your passion for nature (and that is fine), no one is stopping you at home or at week-ends. That is your time to be the nature-loving you. Look forward to the days when you can find people who share your love of this amazing world and spend time with them. You can then relax and do what you love. And doing what you love, with people who understand that, is what life is really about. But I know you know that.

Oh yes—and if a GCSE in Natural History was introduced into schools then young people could learn about nature and not feel side-lined. Wouldn't that be great!

Mary Colwell—TV and radio producer and writer

Wood pigeon
Columba palumbus

Citizen science

Citizen science is exactly what it says on the can, science for the general public. The two main wildlife citizen science surveys that take place each year are the Big Garden Birdwatch and the Big Butterfly Count. Both are incredibly easy—no training is necessary. The data collected provides important information about the state of our garden birds and butterflies.

The Big Garden Birdwatch, run by the RSPB, was started in 1979 as a way to get children involved in a winter weekend activity. Junior members were asked to count the birds in their garden as a way for the RSPB to gather data on the UK's top ten most common garden birds. Now half-a-million people take part, of all ages and backgrounds, and from all over the country, in both urban and rural places. This makes it one of the most popular citizen science projects. It is a pretty simple survey: you just count the species that visit your garden over a period of an hour and fill in the results online.

BLOG (January): Sitting in my kitchen on a freezing January morning with the doors wide open, I am taking part in the annual Big Garden Birdwatch.

It's 8.30 am, there is steam rising from my breakfast sat on the table beside me, my camera is trained on the bird feeder, with a pen and paper ready to note down the species and number of birds that land in my garden.

The normal robin hops along the gate and the dunnock sings its heart out from on top of the clematis. The wood pigeons are obvious, gliding in from the next-door field, scattering the smaller birds that for a split-second must think they are predators.

The long-tailed tits are fairly easy. I can hear them coming with their constant contact calls, which they use to make sure they are all together. They jostle and push but eventually all ten managed to fit onto one feeder.

Two pied wagtails bob along on the path picking up the food that has been knocked off the feeder. The jackdaws noisily arrive, landing in the silver birch tree and, although appearing very boisterous, are actually quite wary, flying down grabbing something and flying back to a safe distance.

All too quickly the hour is up.--**END**

The Big Butterfly Count is run by Butterfly Conservation, launched in 2010. It takes even less time at just 15 minutes. You can take part any day between mid-July and the first week in August. It is as easy as finding a spot and counting the butterflies that you see in 15 minutes. Afterwards, as with the bird survey, you enter the information online.

Butterflies respond very quickly to changes in their environment, which makes them a type of early-warning indicator for possible problems for other wildlife.

Marbled white
Melanargia galathea

BLOG (August): I know a place, it is the simplest of places, not an attractive meadow full of swaying wild flowers but a corner of an arable field. With a hedge on one side, wheat growing across the field to within a metre of where I'm stood next to a patch of thistles, knapp weed, clover and brambles. This place is sheltered from the wind by a wall of discarded hay bales. It is where I have come to do my 15 minutes of counting butterflies.

At least 15 butterflies are flying above or settled on the flowers. They all have their own dance. Some fly straight down, some glide in on the wind in twisting turns, others swooping and rising across the field with a determination at odds with their delicate appearance. Skippers battle over a flower, while large whites spiral up into the air in twos and threes.

I need to remain as still as I can, a single vibration or shadow will send the butterflies scattering.--**END**

We live in turbulent times—during my lifetime over half of the world's wildlife has disappeared. This is incredibly sad but we still have an opportunity to turn the tide and ensure that our wildlife and habitats are better protected in the future. Citizen science—the engagement of the public in providing scientific data—is a great way to achieve this. Knowledge is power and provides an objective assessment of what is happening to the planet. The data that you generate can be used to directly improve environmental management, to enable scientists to provide new insights or to influence policy-makers. In this connected world it has never been easier to mobilise communities to monitor, collate data and protect the environment—so what are you waiting for?

Neil Bailey—EarthWatch Europe

If surveys like these two get you hooked, then there are more in-depth citizen science projects that are either run nationwide or by local groups — such as small mammal surveys — that you can gain experience on while helping alongside experts. These tend to be longer, lasting one or two days.

All information gathered — whether over a short period of time or over years — helps scientists and ecologists collect and then analyse data to understand more about our environment and how we are affecting it.

Some organisations such as ORCA* and EarthWatch† run volunteer vacations where you can pay to go on a sort of working holiday. The organisation and its experts get free help and you get an exciting holiday, experience and learn lots of new stuff. Everybody wins.

My favourite survey is run by ORCA. It is a two-and-a-half day trip from the UK to Santander in Spain and back on a ferry, counting whales and dolphins on the way.

*	ORCA protects whales and dolphins in UK and European waters.
†	Earthwatch engages people worldwide in scientific field research and education to promote the understanding and action necessary for a sustainable environment.

Fin whale
Balaenoptera physalus

BLOG (August): Sat on the deck on Pont Aven, a Brittany ferry bound from Portsmouth to Santander in Spain, I was looking out across miles of blue grey water searching for either a waterspout or a glimpse of a dark grey tail.

Someone shouted 'Whale!' and we all rushed to the side of the ship.

There, around 50m from the port side was a huge fin whale. Even weighing in at around 80 tons this magnificent creature threw itself out of the water surrounded by a cloud of sea spray, much to the amazement of us onlookers.

The excitement of 50 or more people all looking out for whales and shouting out when something is spotted can't be beaten.

At the beginning of the trip we were all strangers to each other, but after three days of education, quizzes, chatting, comparing photographs, as well as synchronised puking from seasickness, by the end of the trip there was lots of swapping names and email addresses.--**END**

Work experience and volunteering

These are two of the best ways to make contacts and get noticed.

Zach—
Young wildlife
enthusiast

Volunteering

Volunteering is both fun and helpful for yourself and good for whoever you volunteer with, especially as some organisations need all the help they can get. Think about what you are interested in. Is it birds, mammals, plants, insects, or maybe one particular species? Ask around and search on social media—many charities will be grateful for some help. Look up your local Wildlife Trust, RSPB site, mammal or bird groups. Some will have a web page about how to become a volunteer, but if not it doesn't hurt to ask them.

Alright, so maybe you will be giving up a lie-in on a Saturday morning or spending the day vegging out in front of a box set, but it will definitely be worth the effort. Not only will the organisations benefit, but you will learn lots in the process, as well as meeting like-minded people. I've had great fun helping out on stalls, with surveys, filming, giving talks and using my knowledge to teach other people about nature. In return I've met ecologists, nature photographers and other people who have an amazing passion for protecting wildlife.

People have given up their time to show me a wide variety of skills, from how to find water voles in vegetation, to gaining the confidence to speak to a crowded room and how to edit video footage. I've had the opportunity to release an injured badger back into the wild, to venture behind the scenes at a natural history museum and see BBC *Springwatch* being filmed.

Work experience

Most teenagers get the chance to do work experience around year 10 — a week in the work place and *away from school!* Lists of the available opportunities are usually posted up, but you may be allowed to find your own placement instead.

Work experience is a chance to find out what options are out there. Think outside the box — working with wildlife isn't just about becoming a warden or making videos: Like any business it could include finance, science, marketing, communications, ecology or campaigning, to name just a few aspects.

For my work experience I was lucky enough to get a week's placement at The Centre for Ecology and Hydrology in Oxfordshire. Over the five days I was there I had the chance to collect river samples for pollution testing, study video of prey being brought into the nest by kestrels and to look at honey collected from all over the world in the lab. The week gave me a great insight into what they get up to at the centre.

Embracing both volunteering and work experience can give you an understanding of what goes on in the workplace and an idea whether it is a career path you want to pursue.

4

GADGETS and technology

What's great about wildlife-watching nowadays is the huge amount of technology that is available to help us. Gone are the days of relying solely on a note pad and pen, welcome to the world of gadgets and apps.

BLOG (May): Sat amongst the bluebells on a late spring evening, a gentle breeze tickling my face. I am waiting for the first black nose to appear out of the ground. It is a moment of excitement, tension and a little bit of apprehension.

Every creature around me is settling down for the night. Blackbirds are singing their final song. Wood pigeons are flapping about high in the branches overhead, looking for their roost for the night.

Through the trees I can see a couple of roe deer silently moving in the dimming light. I hear a rustle, is this a badger? No, much smaller, it's a rat moving through the grass.

In the distance, the church bells are ringing and I can hear the traffic on the dual carriageway, reminding me that I'm not far away from humankind.

Then I hear the first chattering of a badger behind the twisted mess of brambles and I know they are now awake. I slowly adjust my legs and check my camera is on the right settings for the falling light just before the first black and white face appears.

Once one badger emerges, three more follow, then finally, one of this year's cubs appears. Stumbling, unsteady on its feet, this is what I have been waiting to photograph.**--END**

Snorkelling for
underwater photos

Shanny
Lipophrys pholis

Cameras

Where to start?

Compact, bridge, mirrorless or SLR … there are camera shops, magazines and online articles explaining the pros and cons of the different types of cameras. Ask around, read forums, borrow a mate's camera, but choose one you are comfortable with, don't buy one just because it is the latest 'must have'.

It doesn't matter whether you are a Canon convert or a Nikon fanatic — what is important is that you know **how to use** your camera and have fun with it. I read somewhere once, something like 'the best camera is the one you have with you'. No camera in the world is any good sat on a shelf in your bedroom.

Photography is subjective, it is art and, most importantly, a hobby. Yes, there are ways of making your photography better, but enjoy learning. Experiment, the great thing about digital cameras is you can take as many images as your patience can handle looking through later. So, rather than talk cameras, let's talk about **how to take photos**.

Settings

Start off with the auto setting. Get used to your camera, the weight of it, how you hold it, where the buttons and dials are. Can you find the controls without looking or in the dark, or with gloves on?

Where does the lens cap swing when off? Does it knock against your hand annoyingly? How much noise does the mechanism make?

I've been close to buying a particular camera but have been put off by the amount of noise the lens makes as it moves. In short, get to know the capabilities and limitations of your camera. I thought about the time, slowly centimetre by centimetre, crawling along the tractor lines, playing 'grandmothers footsteps' with a hare.

— — — — — — — — — — — — — —

BLOG (July): Lying as flat as I can, face in the mud. Taking a lifetime to remove the lens cap, getting up on my elbows, balancing the camera gradually up to my face, all the while never taking my eye off the hare.

Slowly, slowly, turning the camera on, knowing that any sudden movement will send the hare into the cover of the wheat. It has taken over an hour to get this close, then click, beep, whir, and the hare freezes, muscles clench, ears quiver, then it's GONE.--**END**

— — — — — — — — — — — — — —

Remember to turn all the sounds off!

Pick up your camera, take it outside and play with it until you can use it without having to take your eye off the subject.

I'm not going to repeat what tons of specialist wildlife camera books have said already and talk about shutter speed, ISO and aperture. Instead I suggest you either buy a book, get one from the library or search online for 'basic camera techniques'. For example, *100 Ways to Take Better Nature and Wildlife Photographs* by Guy Edwardes — which I was given by my teachers and governors when I left primary school and which I thoroughly recommend.

Composition

Even if you get all the settings right on your camera, something can make one photo competition-worthy and another one of those that you look at and think 'That's good, but something about it is not quite right'. That could be the composition.

Contrary to what you might think when looking at the awesome photos you see billboard-size at the Natural History Museum it is not that easy to get the best composition when shooting wildlife. It moves!

When you come across an animal performing some amazing behaviour, by the time your brain has decided to take a photo, you've lifted the camera up to your eye and your neurons have sent a message to your finger to press the shutter, that animal can be just a blur in the distance. If luck and fieldcraft (see *page 41*) skills are on your side, the animal wont have seen, heard or smelt you. It will stay still long enough for you to take the photo.

Check out if there is anything annoying in the background, move around or zoom in a little to cut it out. Find the best angle, is that standing or do you need to get down to ground level? Does it look better if the animal is staring straight at you or engaged in an activity?

All these questions are a luxury, sometimes you'll only get a split second to point and shoot. But hopefully with skill, knowledge and a huge amount of luck, the opportunity will be there to take a photo to be proud of.

It seems that every photography article you'll ever read talks about 'rule of thirds'. Your camera probably has the option to show guide lines on the display or viewfinder that you can use to align your subject to produce a balanced and more engaging photograph. But bear in mind, rules are there to be broken and nature is not always obliging.

As well as the lines on your viewfinder, look out for naturally occurring lines, paths, streams, hedgerows or tractor tracks through crops. Whether vertical, horizontal or diagonal, these lines will lead the eye, either creating a more pleasing photo or unintentionally distracting it.

Light

Sunrise and sunset are often mentioned as the best times of day for photography. Life is not that simple though, whoever heard of a teenager wanting to get up early before school?

Nope, it's sleep until the alarm goes, another ten minutes before your mum shouts, another ten minutes until she shouts again, then jump out of bed, grab clothes, breakfast, clean teeth (if your mum catches you) then out of the door hoping the bus hasn't left without you and that you've remembered your PE kit.

Evenings are better. There is nothing more relaxing than the sun setting on another day and heading down into the field, camera in hand, just as the wildlife is settling down or waking up.

— — — — — — — — — — —

BLOG (August): Back against a tree, half dozing as the sun filters its last rays through the trees, I'm watching a roe deer nibbling at bramble leaves. Delicately, she moves slowly, occasionally lifting her head up and sniffing the air, then, satisfied there is no threat she carries on with her evening meal. The sunlight bounces off her grey/brown back highlighting each individual hair.

As each minute brings the sun lower towards the horizon, the deer becomes more and more of a silhouette, a black deer shape against an orange background.--**END**

— — — —

Roe deer
Capreolus capreolus

The light is important with wildlife photography but don't get hung up about it. Nature creates some awesome light whatever the conditions. Just think of that purple right before a thunderstorm or the dapple of sunlight through leaves. Even on the dullest of grey days you can experiment with light using your imagination.

Spider on wheat

Trail cameras

One of my favourite bits of kit and a regular substitute if I can't get out with my camera is the trail camera. The trail camera or camera trap is a must-have for everyone interested in wildlife watching.

These marvellous devices will film or take photos when you are not around — giving an insight into behaviour that might be different to that when an animal senses someone is watching them. How cool is that?

Trail cameras work using a PIR **sensor** (the same thing security lights and burglar alarms use) which 'trips' when a creature passes through close enough to the camera. Some more advanced devices will also have a setting called **'Field Scan'** which takes a photo at a pre-set time.

A trail camera gives you an opportunity to see into a world that is often hidden from us, at night, in awkward places or just because putting in the hours with school and other commitments is impossible to do.

They come in a range of prices from supermarket budget cameras to the more expensive models with interchangeable lenses, no-show LEDs and viewfinders. Find the one that works for you and your budget and you'll soon be hooked and looking to upgrade.

TOP TIP: Either wear gloves when handling the trail camera, or smear some mud onto it from the area around where you are leaving it. Then mammals won't be wary of the smell.

If you're dead skint, look at **borrowing** one off a mate. Some local groups have trail cameras that you can hire until you decide whether they are worth the money (or your next birthday or payday comes around).

I also use mine as an extra fieldcraft tool, by leaving a trail camera in the same place for a week or so. This allows me to work out **patterns of behaviour** and times certain animals visit a particular place. By moving the camera around I can get a fair idea of an individual animal's territory.

It takes a while to get used to using a trail camera and it will take a few days for the animals — particularly mammals — to get comfortable with it being there too.

Once you've worked out all the different settings (if you can play on an Xbox a trail camera is a pushover) next thought is **where to put it**. Look for signs of animals, their trails, their homes or places you've seen them before. Next, look at the height and the angle. If there is foliage in the way either move the camera higher or change angle. Objects that are too close will cause 'flash glare' and it'll look like you've filmed a ghost.

Best trick for the **focus**, especially if you have an interchangeable lens, is to use a ruler or pre-measured bit of string to determine the distance between the camera and where you guess the animal is going to pass. This is because the camera will have a fixed range between which anything should be in focus, and outside of which (too close or too far away) things will be blurred. At first there will be lots of video of tails, legs and out of focus faces. But with more practice and a bit of luck there will be some amazing surprises to be seen.

Oh and don't forget to **lock the camera up**, I use a cycle chain lock.

To love nature, you have to experience it...to listen to a dawn chorus on a frosty morning, to stand in dark woodland whilst a tawny's call pierces the night air, to soak up the magical atmosphere in a summer meadow. Aim to spend some of every day outside...the more you do it the more you will want to do it!

Start by attracting wildlife to you... from a tiny window box to a single bird feeder, this is your portal to nature. And nature will be your inspiration, your medicine, your escape and your joy!

In a world dominated by material items and money, I strongly believe the best things in life are free! From a stroll in the park to a mountain adventure, getting outside and learning to get immersed in the natural world is good for the mind and soul...so what's your excuse? Get out there!

Kate MacRae — Wildlife Kate, wildlife enthusiast, blogger, teacher, photographer and trail camera addict

Smartphones

Most of us carry some sort of phone with us every second of every day. Whether you see it as necessary or a burden, make the most of it. Most phones now have fairly decent cameras, which you can add lenses to, such as macro, wide angled, or even fish eye, making 'mobiography' highly accessible and popular. Together with decent capabilities, lenses and the ability to edit and post to social media in an instant, smartphones are portable, always to-hand and are increasingly producing amazing art.

GoPro and action cameras

Both GoPro and their equivalents are the cameras of adventure. Small, robust, action cameras that you can attach to your bike, kayak, yourself, your dog — your imagination is the only limit. They can film the coolest exploits: jumping into water, cycling downhill or running through a wood.

With their compact size and weighing only around 150 grammes these durable, resilient cameras are stress-free to use (especially if you invest in one with a screen) and easy to throw in a pocket or rucksack and take away with you. They are waterproof or come with a waterproof housing, giving you a whole new level of awesome opportunities to film in or near water.

The awe-inspiring range of accessories means you can, for example, attach them to your chest or head and operate them hands-free, or put them on a pole for extra reach and distance. Lay it in the grass or attach to a tree for a different perspective.

Amateurs and professionals alike use these cameras. Check out YouTube for some breathtaking examples of what these action cameras can do. Don't forget they take pretty good stills as well as video. They have even been used to win major wildlife photography competitions, for example Tim Laman's shot of an orangutan for Wildlife Photographer of the Year 2016.

Time-lapse

Time-lapse is incredible for showing what happens over a long period of time in just a few seconds or minute. We've all seen those amazing videos where someone has taken one selfie a day for a whole year, then put together a film of how they've changed (if not, have a look!).

Well, the technique is also one of the tricks of the trade in wildlife filming. It is great for subjects such as changing seasons, growing plants, sunsets and the incoming tide. The list is only limited by your imagination.

Some bridge and DSLR cameras have the ability or you can invest in a dedicated time-lapse camera. The only fiddly bit is working out the right frames-per-second setting to use. Generally the best time lapse has thirty pictures (or 'frames') played in one second. This is usually abbreviated to *30f/sec.* This gives a smooth looking video.

1 Choose how long you are going to film your subject for. For example, a growing plant could be for one week, whereas the moon rising could be filmed over three hours.

2 Next decide how often you want to take a photo. For example, a plant isn't going to change much every minute, so you could set the camera to take a photo every 30 minutes.

3 Lastly think about how long your audience will want to view the final video clip for. No-one is going to sit and watch time lapse for ten minutes.

You'll need to play around with the settings, but here are some examples to get you started (the algebra you learnt in school that you never thought you would use, does come in handy):

Subject	Time* (T)	Interval* (I)	Frame rate (R)	Calculation $T \times I \div R = L$	Video length (L)
Moon rising	3 hours (180 mins)	30 secs (2 per minute)	30	$180 \times 2 \div 30 = 12$	12 seconds
Flowers growing**	1 week (168 hours)	30 mins (2 per hour)	30	$168 \times 2 \div 30 = 11.2$	11 seconds
Bird eggs hatching	15 minutes	5 secs (12 per min)	30	$15 \times 12 \div 30 = 6$	6 seconds

Example calculations for time-lapse photography

* For the calculation to work you need to use the same time unit for Time (T) and Interval (I) — both minutes, or both hours — but it doesn't matter which.

** You'll need to decide whether you will still want to film overnight, in which case you'll just need to edit out the dark parts.

Bat detectors

There are several types of bat detector:
- Tunable heterodyne detectors
  (like the one in the blog post below);
- Time expansion detectors;
- Frequency division detectors.

Numerous groups advertise bat watching evenings. At these, Wildlife Trust experts can show you how to use a bat detector and point out how to recognise different bats. They do this not only using a bat detector but by the bats' behaviour, size, flight pattern and wing shape.

— — — — — — — — — — — — —

BLOG (July): The sky is rapidly turning from bright turquoise to a midnight blue. One-by-one stars appear, creating recognisable patterns overhead such as The Plough.

To the background of gentle chatter and cutlery chinking that belongs to the summer party, small black objects dart amongst the trees. One of my mate's dads shouts out that he has a bat detector in the house, people look up and shrug, but a few of us show interest.

After a little bit of fiddling around with the tuning dial, down at the bottom of the garden, away from the party and the lights, a group of us listen to the tiny clicks coming from the plastic box each time one of the small black shapes passes overhead.

Incredible to think each click is a translation of the high-pitched calls, mostly inaudible to humans, that the bats use to create a 'sound picture' of their surroundings using echolocation.

Each bat species makes a different call at different frequencies. The bat detector enabled the group of us at the party to determine that the nocturnal hunters feeding on the gnats, midges and mosquitoes over our heads were pipistrelle bats.**--END**
— — — — — — — — — — — —

Apps and websites

Every one of us uses apps and websites, if we don't know something we 'Google it'. It is second nature to our generation. There are some fantastic apps out there and, even better, most of them are free.

You can get apps for identifying species, recording data and learning more information while out in the field, and there are websites for editing, researching and exchanging information when you get back home. Spend some time looking out for apps that suit your interests the best. Most are free to download. Here are a few of my favourites.

Big Butterfly Count

This app is linked to the annual citizen science event of the same name. It has information on how to get involved in the count and tables of first sightings for the year. During July and August you can use the app to upload your sightings on the go.

Pocket Pals

This is a game based around wildlife found in the UK, set up by university students Dani Connor and Matt Brown. Players walk around and locate digital animals, using GPS. In doing so, the player will learn how to identify and classify British animals from mammals to insects, while also gaining knowledge on their habitat and behaviour. The aim is to connect players with wildlife.

Nature Finder

This is an app created by the Wildlife Trusts. It helps you locate nearby nature reserves all over the UK as well as keeping you up-to-date with events. You can find out what you are likely to see at each reserve, any restrictions such as disabled access, whether dogs are allowed or if they have a café.

The Great British Bee Count

Similar to the butterfly app, this links to a citizen science project. With this one if you aren't brilliant at telling your honey bee from your mason bee you can take a photo and upload it. It has an added quirk of 'buzzing' like a bee when you open the app. From Friends of the Earth.

OS Maps

This Ordnance Survey app is an extension to their paper maps. When you buy a printed map you get a code to type into OS Maps, making it viewable on your phone (even offline). Great if you don't want to be folding and unfolding a map every few minutes. It is available on two levels: Free gives you the standard map and the ability to plan and record routes. If you pay for a monthly subscription (which covers all your devices) you get offline access to all maps plus the added bonus of the Explorer and Landranger maps with extra features and augmented reality.

5

Get
COMPETITIVE

Autumnal fungi

It's time to get your hard work out there and noticed. It's competition time! Sort through your favourite photos and try entering them into some contests. Many of the main comps have under-18 sections that are free to enter, so what have you got to lose?

But how do you choose which photographs to enter? I don't have a simple answer to that one, as like other art it is all very subjective. What I like might not be what you like, or the judges like. That doesn't mean you've not got a great photo, just that individuals connect with different images. Look through your photos and shortlist the ones you keep going back to, the really pin sharp ones, the photos that *tell a story*.

Get some mates round, grab a pizza and make an evening of it. You can each give different points of view. Your friends might see something in a photo that you don't. You can help each other decide which images to submit. You can have an amazing technically perfect photo but if it doesn't grab you then what is it worth?

7-spot ladybird
Coccinella septempunctata

TOP TIP:
Look online at previous winners and runners up. Note the standard of entries and the type of thing the judges are looking for.

Entering your hard-won images into competitions can be a fun way of getting feedback on your work, recognition of the time and effort you might have put into studying your subject, and a great pointer for your future wildlife projects.

Some people think that to 'wow' the judges you have to have something new that they may not have seen before. This is sometimes true, but equally likely to be successful are images that show common subjects in a new light, or that perfectly capture the character of the animal in its natural surroundings.

Remember, judges are always looking out for outstanding images but they must be technically proficient too!

Dan Bolt—Award-winning underwater photographer

103

With any competition — enter for fun. It's awesome to be short-listed or even to win but don't get hung up about it. If you don't get anywhere, it may just be that your entry wasn't what the judges were looking for this time around. Perhaps you entered a shot of a deer but so did 50 other people when only two people submitted a photo of a water vole. It is the luck of the draw sometimes and even top, well-known photographers don't win every competition they enter.

Don't stress, if you really think you have a winning photo, just enter it into a different competition. There are hundreds out there run by anything from small local camera clubs to regional Wildlife Trusts to worldwide organisations.

Not great at photography? Don't want to spend your time learning? Feel your talents lie elsewhere? No worries. Look out for competitions such as those for paintings or other artwork.

Some of these contests will predominantly be aimed at adults with a child or young adult category. Others may be general artwork or painting competitions with a wildlife theme one year or the option to enter any subject you choose, which could include nature or wildlife.

The RSPB runs a competition called WildArt for anyone 19 years or under. There is also the major 'Wildlife Artist of the Year' — run by The David Shepherd Wildlife Foundation — and even if you don't think you are up to that standard it's definitely worth looking at the entries for inspiration.

What if you are better at writing? Keep an eye out for poetry or storytelling competitions. As with art, they may be general contests into which you could enter a nature-based poem or story. The Barn Owl Trust has been running an annual wildlife poetry competition for a number of years.

If making videos is more your thing or you have a message you want to get across that needs more than a photo, a painting or a poem, then try your hand at some of the short film competitions. New ones pop up every year and there are old favourites such as the RSPB's Cairngorms Nature Young Presenter. Filming things is a great way to get others involved with you — you'll need someone to star in your production!

James Miller
RSPB Cairngorms
Nature Young Presenter

Here are a few tips

- Sign up to newsletters, you'll then get notifications of opening and closing dates;
- Read the terms and conditions carefully, you don't want a brilliant photo or story disqualified because it was sent in the wrong format or had a couple of words too many;
- Don't rule out international competitions. As long as you meet the criteria, you have as much chance of winning as anyone does;
- Check out previous winners to see the standard of entries.

Some of the more popular competitions

- Wildlife Photographer of the Year;
- British Wildlife Photography Awards;
- Bird Photographer of the Year Awards;
- Mammal Photographer of the Year;
- RSPB Kids (various competitions in poetry, art and sound);
- National Geographic Kids (various contests throughout the year).

Get competitive and good luck!

European robin
Erithacus rubecula

6
JUGGLING wildlife and your life

Dealing with time

With any hobby, finding the time to fit it in can sometimes prove difficult. I'm the type of person who likes to come home from school, with the weekend stretching out in front of me, dump my school bags down, grab a snack and my camera then head out into the woods to see what's around. All the while trying to put thoughts of homework to the back of my head.

This is much to the exasperation of my parents who end up pulling their hair out on Sunday afternoons because I'm struggling with a piece of maths or need to go to the shops to get something for a project.

Young rabbit
Orytolagus cuniculus

I looked online at lots of memes about life, time management and wildlife photography and that put off at least an hour of writing this paragraph. Time management is not my strong point!

The best thing about wildlife is that it is everywhere, so even if you haven't got time to put aside specifically to watch it there are still plenty of opportunities. While out shopping there are always birds and insects around. Those starlings, gulls and rooks that hang around car parks at retail outlets are fascinating to watch. Their presence and behaviour is so often ignored. Lunch breaks, travelling home from school and long car journeys all provide opportunities for a spot of unplanned wildlife watching.

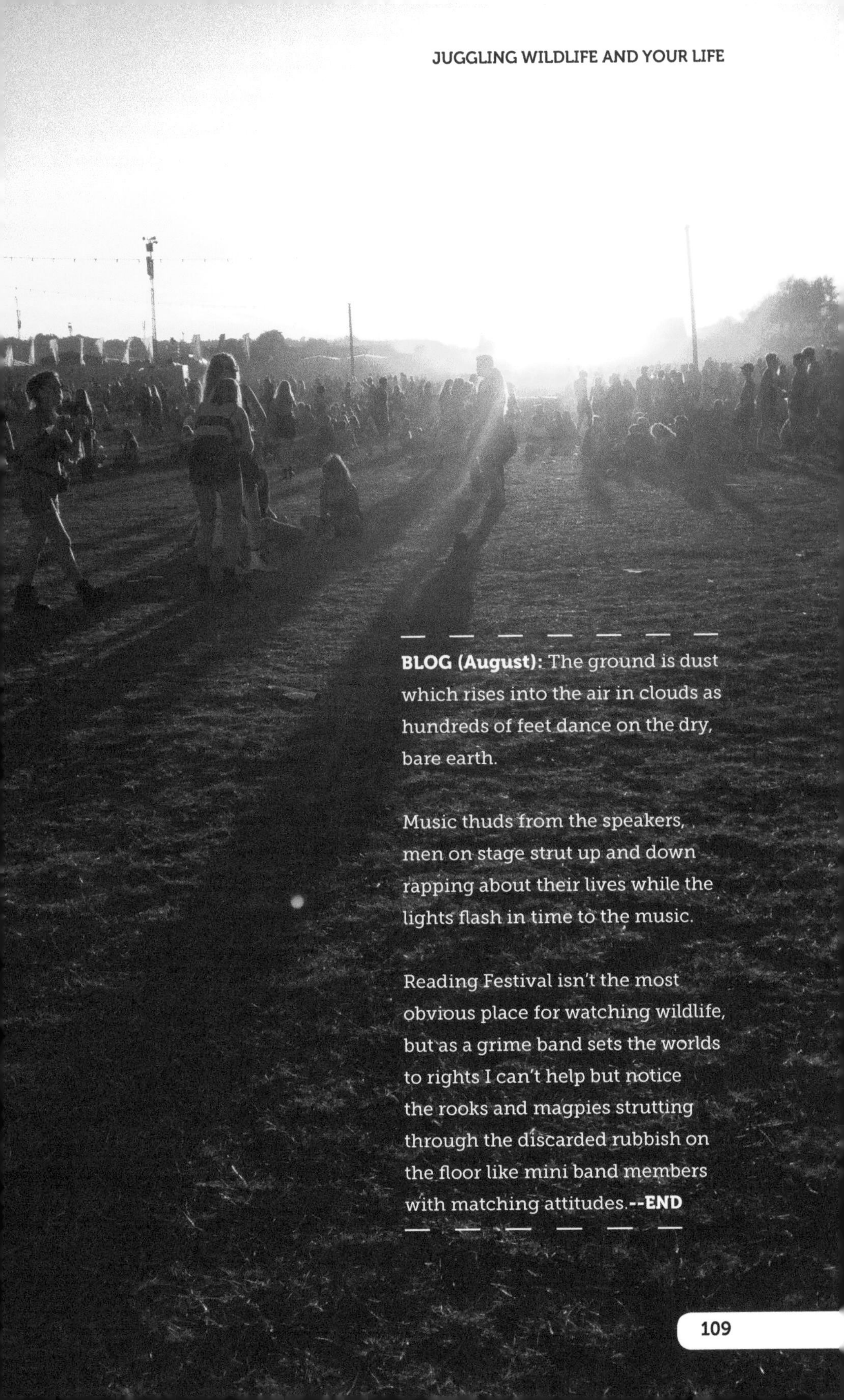

BLOG (August): The ground is dust which rises into the air in clouds as hundreds of feet dance on the dry, bare earth.

Music thuds from the speakers, men on stage strut up and down rapping about their lives while the lights flash in time to the music.

Reading Festival isn't the most obvious place for watching wildlife, but as a grime band sets the worlds to rights I can't help but notice the rooks and magpies strutting through the discarded rubbish on the floor like mini band members with matching attitudes.**--END**

The Wildlife Trusts 30 Days Wild has some excellent ideas for mini wildlife moments that run throughout the month of June, from doing homework in the garden to bike rides with your mates. Check out www.wildlifetrusts.org

For when you still need that wildlife fix but time is short, trail cameras can do the work for you (see *page 92*). They will check out what is going on when you can't be there.

Buzzard
Buteo buteo

Exam tips

As schoolwork increases and exams approach, time for wildlife-watching shrinks, but I think it is important to squeeze in a bit of nature whenever you can:

- Take a five minute break every hour — set a timer and walk to the bottom of the garden, clear your head, breathe and stop thinking about exams for 300 seconds;
- Exercise is good for your brain, so start the day with a brief wildlife walk. Just limit yourself to 20-30 mins before you get stuck into your revision;
- Organise study groups with friends — meet up somewhere quiet outdoors;
- Remember to drink plenty of water and eat healthy snacks;
- Reward yourself with some time outside once you've finished for the day.

ACTIVISM

7

Get off your backside

I'm scrolling through my social media accounts finding it incredibly hard to look at some of the feeds. Canned hunting, badger baiting, culls, raptor persecution, wildlife crime and falling numbers of certain species, it all appears before my eyes on a regular basis. A lump is rising in my throat, my chest feels tight, and I feel totally useless. What can we do?

Firstly, don't just scroll past it, as hard as that may be. If it is something that you feel strongly about or you had no idea such things were happening, research into it a bit more. Find out the details, the reasons why. If it is still hitting you right in the chest, share the post with others — the more people that know about it, the more people may recognise a sign on their local patch. For example:

- A couple of cars in a lay-by at the side of a field may mean hare coursing;
- A dog walking through a town covered in cuts may mean it has been used in dog fighting.

It may be innocent, but then again it may not be. Wildlife crime is any action that contravenes current legislation governing the protection of wild animals and plants.

Riders participating in a legal trail hunt

Recognise, record and report

Partnership for Action Against Wildlife Crime UK (PAW UK) is an agency made up of organisations involved in wildlife law enforcement. It's sponsored by the Department for Food, Environment & Rural Affairs (Defra). It represents around 100 organisations whose collective aim is to raise awareness of wildlife legislation and the impacts of wildlife crime, help and advise on it and make sure it is tackled effectively.

Birders Against Wildlife Crime has a motto: Recognise, record and report. Take the time to learn what signs to **recognise**, **record** all the details down, no matter how insignificant they may seem. Finally **report**: if it is a crime in progress then phone 999; if it is something that has already happened then phone 101 or your local Wildlife Crime Officer (see nwcu.police.uk).

Something you feel strongly about may not always be illegal. It may be something that a company, your local council or even the national government are doing, but they might not realise how strongly the general public feel against it, or are unwilling to find a more sensible solution. This is where action like signing petitions or writing to MPs can make a difference. Initiatives such as Surfers Against Sewage and the League Against Cruel Sports were set up because somebody felt something needed to be done.

While my teenage years are long (long) behind me, they do still shape how I think about wildlife and how I (sometimes) relate to other people.

I remember an almost complete indifference to wildlife from my school friends. Wildlife was already a 'way of life' to me. I thought about it all the time. I even set up a school natural history magazine with one of the very few other animal nuts I knew (who, incidentally, went on to work for the BBC Natural History Unit producing series including Blue Planet and Planet Earth). The magazine didn't last long, but we tried. Even forty years ago I wanted to explain why birds fascinated me and why I wanted to help protect them.

And that's how it's been ever since. A series of different approaches to convince an apparently disinterested public that wildlife matters, that we are the environment just as much as the trees and the animals we walk past every day, that what we do and how we think is important. In many ways my teenage self hasn't really changed, and neither—to a large extent—has public attitude.

My teenage self experienced isolation, some mockery, large doses of apathy, but the joy I found in wildlife, the beauty I discovered, the fire nature ignited made up for all of that. I don't suppose for a moment that my experiences are wholly different to those of today's teenagers who are going through the same battles with friends and society in general (though the sense of urgency is undoubtedly more strongly felt). But a major difference is that they have each other, an online network to turn to, and more opportunities than ever to make their voice heard. And—if they choose to use them—a generation of conservationists who know how hard it is to make a difference at an age when you probably feel at your most enthusiastic and passionate.

Charlie Moores—Campaigner, podcaster and
Vice-Chair, League Against Cruel Sports

Getting involved

There are plenty of ways to get involved, starting right at home by signing online petitions, joining in thunderclaps and writing to your member of parliament (MP). You may feel that some of these don't work, but just sharing and informing others is a great start.

Thunderclaps are a mass-shared single message which are great in today's social media dominated world, where posts disappear so quickly. These flash-mob type posts bombard Twitter, Facebook, Instagram, etc. with the same message at exactly the same moment to create maximum impact.

With online petitions, once they reach 100,000 signatures then they will get a chance to be debated in Parliament. Whether it goes further than that is dependent on many things.

Your MP is supposed to be there to represent the people living in his or her constituency. They must advocate and promote the interests of the people that they serve, whether or not they actually voted for them. They aren't supposed to just push their own views. It is worth writing to them if you feel strongly about something that is going on in your local area or that is to be debated in Parliament. You can find out who your local MP is at: parliament.uk/mps-lords-and-offices/mps/

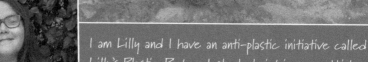

I am Lilly and I have an anti-plastic initiative called Lilly's Plastic Pickup. I started picking up rubbish when I was walking with my grandpa and was learning to speak Dutch as we had just moved to Holland. I counted 91 pieces of rubbish and thought 'Should I be mad or sad about this?'. Grandpa told me that anything thrown on the ground will somehow make its way to the water-ways and ultimately the sea. I learnt then about the plastic soup and thought I have to do my best to keep the plastic out of the ocean.

I pick up and then sort my pickups into paper, cans, glass, and plastic and take a picture and put it on Facebook. Since the pictures of my pickups have been on social media I have had many videos made of me, and these have been translated and sent to many countries in the world.

I am youth ambassador for the Plastic Pollution Coalition and world charity HOW Global. I do my best to encourage people to refuse single use plastic. I have my own reusable bamboo straw and spork set that I can use instead of accepting disposable ones.

I was invited to the Plastic Whale Conference in Norway to do a big shoreline clean up and talk about plastic pollution with other environ-mentalists and politicians. I was also invited to meet the conservationist Dame Jane Goodall in London and will meet her again when she comes to Holland.

Lilly—Environmental champion and creator of #lillysglobalcleanupday

Protesting

The next step is joining a peaceful protest. These can be marches or gatherings outside a company or building.

BLOG (July): Walking through the streets surrounded by people dressed in black and white. Signs, flags and banners are proudly held high in the sky.

Hundreds are joining in the chant that has followed the Badger Army around the country over the past few years 'Save our Badgers, Stop the Cull!'. Familiar faces nod and smile, as many of us are returning for a third year.

As we walk through the busy Saturday shopping areas, some people take leaflets, stop and talk. They are totally unaware that there is a badger cull. A few people shout abuse and I wonder if they agree with the badger cull or are just trying to impress the group they stand with. Some cars drive past beeping the horn, people waving in agreement with us.

When the march finally reaches the park, badger masks and costumes are removed and banners are laid on the ground. The speeches start, along with photographs being taken, tweets tweeted and social media begins to show the watchers that there are people out here that are willing to give up their time for something they believe in.

Georgia —
Young wildlife
enthusiast

Other ways

In the UK we are lucky enough to be able to show our feelings through peaceful protests. Some people feel that letter writing and marches aren't enough for them and prefer to get directly involved. This doesn't mean doing anything illegal or violent:

- For those over the age of 16 there are activities such as hunt monitoring or the Wounded Badger Patrol;
- For those younger, volunteering on stalls to spread a message is always welcome and a great way to get involved and meet others who have the same interests.

Whatever platform you choose to use to make your feelings known, Anneka Svenska has a few wise words about staying polite, safe and legal.

You are never too young to defend wildlife and animals in our country. It's important to do it the right way though and be safe. I have been speaking at protests for several years now, but there are many things to think about before you take that step and venture out.

If you are under 16, make sure you are accompanied by a responsible adult known to you, better that it's a close family friend or relative who can keep you safe, as some protests can get crowded and, let's face it, you are often in the heart of London.

Think about what the protest is about. Is it a proper protest run by a reputable organisation/charity or will it be anarchic and possibly violent? If it's the latter, you would be far safer not attending and also, if you want to make a career in wildlife, to muddy your name with violent protests is not going to help your reputation at the BBC Wildlife Unit.

Think about what you will wear and the message you would like to get across. You can dress up and your banner can send a powerful message that could be picked up by the press or photographers. As you get older, you can always ask the organisers if they will allow you to speak. I know that charities are always looking for the next up and coming animal defenders.

Finally, bring a good camera or film segments on your phone—this will be great to use to build a wildlife/political blog and, over time, this can contribute to an online biography and CV. Just remember, if you want a career working with animals, always be respectful in how you act and how you speak about others. You may feel strongly about a subject, but there are great ways to get this across without the use of foul language, offending races and countries. You never know, you could be the next Chris Packham or Dominic Dyer.

Anneka Svenska—Wildlife presenter and conservationist

Whalefest

The internet, particularly social media, is a great way to find out how to join in at whatever level you feel is right for you. Whether your passion is wildlife in general or a particular species that you want to protect, there is a group out there who will be extremely grateful for any help you can offer.

It would be wrong of me to pretend that my childhood was filled with the wonderment of nature. I was fortunate to grow up in the Yorkshire Dales, surrounded by natural beauty, but I suppose in reality I took it for granted; always aware of my surroundings, but never truly conscious of the need to protect and learn about them. How my mind-set has changed over the years! Now I see it as my number one priority to take action against those who seek to harm these wonderful habitats and their occupants. If I have a regret, it's that I didn't get involved in the protection of wildlife when I was a teenager. It's never too soon to take action. My campaigns with Sea Shepherd have taken me to some amazing places in the quest to prevent poaching and the illegal harming of our oceans, perhaps our most valuable wildlife resource.

Mark Muschamp—Wildlife activist and senior volunteer with Sea Shepherd

8

Next
GENERATION

We are the future

Here comes the serious bit ... Our generation will be the next decision-makers, scientists, business people, employers and employees, volunteers and citizens. It is down to us to make a difference, to ask questions.

Questions such as: *Why do we tolerate single-use items? Why are we using so many chemicals?* Or *Why do we waste so much food?*

In fact *Why wait?* These are questions we can ask **now**. Question your school, your parents and your friends.

During 2017 I made a short film that was shown to local business people, planning officers and conservationists from Oxfordshire. I was keen to demonstrate to them how much I care about nature and wildlife, I was hoping that my words might be listened to and might even make a difference, even if only to one person.

Prof David Macdonald (Professor of Wildlife Conservation at Oxford University), Alex and Dr Ben Garrod (Professor of Evolutionary Biology and Science Engagement at the University of East Anglia)

Nature is extremely important to me, it is a huge part of my life, and it is my way of feeling connected to the world around me.

I can watch the seasons change all over Oxfordshire, and within those seasons I notice the comings and goings of different animals, plants and birds.

Nature is my escape from a world that has become dominated by electronic devices, from the pressures of teenage life. It is my way of chilling out after a day at school.

For my generation there are lots of pressures. As young people we have stress from school work, teachers, parents and exams, and especially from a world full technology.

We can easily become caught up a virtual reality world, sitting in our bedrooms taking part in online group chats or games with people from anywhere in the world rather than having actual face-to-face contact. This makes connections with nature so important for our sanity and physical health.

My generation are the future and there are plenty of us who care about nature, both locally and around the country. It is unthinkable that during the last ten years we have lost numerous species and at this rate by the time I have children of my own we could lose such amazing creatures as dormice, turtle doves and the hedgehog.

Nature is hugely important to me, to my generation, to your generation and to everyone on the planet. Oxfordshire holds a fantastic array of wildlife that ranges from resident mammals to migratory birds. Extending from farmland, to lakes, to woodland through to urban gardens, Oxfordshire is truly an amazing place for wildlife.

Personally I particularly value the larger mammals. To stumble across a deer or a hare while out on a walk or to find a hedgehog pottering around in my garden is better than any TV show (sorry *Springwatch*).

Then there are the magnificent birds of prey circling the Oxfordshire skies, from the success story of the red kite to the visitors such as the hobby or the short-eared owl. But my overall favourite species has to be the badger.

Nature in the UK is faring worse than in many other countries, with 56% of species in decline. Along with the rest of the UK, nature in Oxfordshire is under threat.

Wildlife and its habitats are under threat from the way we manage our land, from monoculture to extensive building. Losing our woodlands and flower meadows, building roads and the fragmentation of the land all put animals at risk.

While we all have to eat and have to have somewhere to live there has to be consideration for the fellow creatures that we share our land with.

During my time of being interested in wildlife I have become concerned about two species in particular, not what you might call exciting or exotic species but creatures that most of you would think as being 'common'.

Both the house sparrow and the hedgehog have seriously declined in my lifetime, to the point that they could be in serious trouble.

Up until last year I had never seen a hedgehog in the wild. Then last summer one arrived in our garden. Within a few weeks, that hedgehog had two hoglets of her own. I spent evening after evening watching them snuffle around eating slugs and the hedgehog food I put out for them. Each night they would come back for the water I left out. It would be a huge shame to see such an iconic native creature disappear from Oxfordshire and the rest of the UK.

Each and every one of us can do something, no matter how small, to help nature and the environment. On an individual level we can do small things such as leaving out fresh water. We can create hedgehog highways through our gardens. To us these may seem insignificant acts but to wildlife it could be a matter of life or death.

There are some fantastic examples out there of nature-friendly schemes from wildlife corridors, to sustainable farming schemes, to environmentally-friendly buildings and green homes to the reintroduction of localised extinct animals, for example the success story of the red kite.

Corridors = 'Passages' wildlife can use to move between wild areas separated by urban spaces

I would like to see much more education on nature in schools. How can we care about something we know nothing about and therefore have no connection to?

I would like to see all MPs — from every party — pledge to do more for the environment. No matter whether you are an individual or head of a multi-million pound company, an MP or a planning officer, I would like to ask you to have a little more consideration for nature.

We only get one chance at this; hopefully it is not too late to change the state of nature to a positive.

There are so many people out there that are an inspiration to me and I hope that in turn my generation can also be an inspiration to those that follow us.

Inspiring just one youngster is to me worth infinitely more than influencing a hundred adult minds. I wish I knew how to make the natural world a popular topic across all age groups. It would probably solve the world's problems in one go!

Stephen de Vere—British wildlife film-maker and cameraman

After school

'What do you want to do when you grow up?', or 'What are you going to do when you leave school?' are two of the most frequently asked questions kids hear. Some people know exactly what they want to be when they are older from a very young age, others have a rough idea that they may finalise or change slightly, while others have no idea at all and are happy to see where life takes them.

I chose my GCSE 'options' with the idea that I want to do something connected with wildlife but as I write I don't know whether I'll do A-Levels, a BTEC, go to university or do an apprenticeship. As I have not yet experienced life after school, I have enlisted a few of my older friends to tell you where their path led them.

Meadow grasshopper
Chorthippus parallelus

Blue tit
Cyanistes caeruleus

Garden snail
Cornu aspersum

University

University is great for acquiring a degree, but also helping you step into the working world. It provides valuable contacts, especially those who studied a different course to you. Falmouth University was my first choice to apply for as it provided a wide range of technology from large 5×4 bellows film cameras all the way to Hasselblad Medium format. The facilities included our own lab full of microscopes, multiple fully-equipped studios and film processing for both black and white and colour. But the best of the best had to be our access to underwater camera setups worth £12,000 a go.

The university is well known by the BBC and many professional photographers come to talk about their experiences and adventures. Two of my favourite speakers were journalist Sophie Stafford (one of my idols) and Alex Tattersall (an incredible experimental photographer who loves showing off Nauticam's latest toys!). Falmouth has much success at giving people the tools to follow their dreams, such as Jacky Poon who now heads out to photograph snow leopards. He also presented in a documentary on snub nose macaques, which was the first of its kind. As a past graduate of Falmouth University he remains in contact to provide talks to current students.

Falmouth is known for its amazing wildlife reserves and provides great opportunities for diving. The course included many trips such as to the Galápagos to study the wildlife, Egypt to dive the beautiful clear water and the Cairngorms to camp and wake up to grouse and wild hare at the doorstep!

A good tip from a lecturer was: 'Always say yes to opportunities that arise, to go travelling or to volunteer to look after monkeys for a year (for example), as that could be the start of something great, a kick-start to your wildlife careers.' I have been following this tip and I have never regretted a single thing.

Robyn Winfield studied Marine and Natural History Photography at Falmouth University. She then travelled and built up her portfolio. She is currently a wildlife photographer on land and underwater.

Weasel
Mustela nivalis

Beyond school life

I had no idea at Alex's age that I wanted a career in nature conservation. I stayed in education and completed A-Levels because that's what everyone I knew was doing, and I chose the subjects I liked best — Geography, Biology and Sport & PE (plus an AS-Level in Business Studies, which was not for me!). I then went on to do a BSc in Geography at the University of Sussex — a location chosen primarily for its proximity to the sea. I'd always spent a lot of time outdoors growing up in Devon and Cornwall, but wasn't particularly into wildlife until this point. I ended up choosing mostly ecology and conservation modules, and it was some time during my degree that I realised my dream job was in conservation.

Soon after graduating, I started a full time, unpaid role as a Trainee Ranger with East Sussex County Council for a year. I was fortunate (and still am!) to have the financial and emotional support of my mum, which is obviously not an option for everyone. I also worked at a variety of part time jobs — from cleaner to football match hostess — to fund this, and somehow still found time to have a social life. I knew very little in terms of practical conservation at this point, but my academic background provided a solid base to learn from. I feel like I've learnt things every day from this time

(2011) on, and think and hope that will continue for the rest of my life! I feel that the phrase 'The more you know the more you know how little you know' is very true in conservation. Although this might be partly because I want to know about as much as possible! For example, last night I stayed up late completing an online course called 'Understanding Autism'—relevant as I work with a broad range of people. And I'm currently writing this on the train to a 'Learn To Love Centipedes, Millipedes and Woodlice' course (both relevant to my jobs, but done in my free time).

My work includes practical conservation, community engagement and biological recording. One day I might be leading a wildlife club for families, the next I could be felling trees with a chainsaw and then planning a large bioblitz event. It may well be a simpler and quicker route to a paid job if you specialise, but I love doing a bit of everything. My journey has been long—rewarding largely but also very stressful at times. This wasn't helped by a prolonged period of ill health.

After completing my traineeship in Sussex, I spent the next three years volunteering part time and working part time in vaguely-related paid jobs (including for a carbon reduction company and with a tree surgeon). I spent a lot of time and energy applying for jobs in conservation with no success. In 2015 I got a place on the South West Wildlife Trusts' Wildlife Skills project, supported by the Heritage Lottery Fund with not only a training budget but also a monthly grant for living costs. In my opinion, securing a place on a project like this is one of the best routes into a career in nature conservation. Following this, I moved around the country for a couple of short term contracts before ending up in my current jobs, which are both permanent and part time. My journey hasn't been the most straightforward, but I've learnt so much along the way and am happy where I am now.

Charley Miller is Conservation and Education Coordinator at Hazel Hill Trust, Wiltshire; Community Wildlife Assistant at Berkshire, Buckinghamshire and Oxfordshire Wildlife Trust and Mentoring Coordinator at A Focus on Nature (the UK's youth nature network).

Common lizard
Zootoca vivipara

My career path

Before progressing onto Higher Education from Further Education, I volunteered for the RSPB in Birmingham. It gave me an insight into the various job roles there are and knowledge of specific wildlife in and around where I am from. For their *A Date With Nature* events, I assisted with passing on knowledge of local wildlife, such as the plight of the once ubiquitous house sparrow and of how peregrines were breeding, nesting and hunting in the city centre. Plus selling pin-badges and memberships. This gave me experience in engaging with the public and meeting people from all backgrounds, with different opinions, levels of knowledge and ages.

During the summer I observed and filmed a grey squirrel family in their drey, which was inside the roof of my neighbour's garage, by discreetly installing a mini wireless camera. It was rather exciting, seeing the secret goings on and I wanted to share it with others, so I contacted BBC Birmingham and I did a write up on my experience for of it for their website and soon after I was interviewed for the BBC *Midlands Today* news programme by the Environment Correspondent, Dr David Gregory-Kumar.

If you would like to go to university, then I suggest you find the one that suits you best; one with a course that meets your needs, no matter how far away from where you grew up it is and it doesn't have to be one your friends or boyfriend/girlfriend are going to either.

Personally, I didn't go to university, I opted to do a Higher National Diploma (HND) at a local college, because at the time (2008-2010) the media (Moving Image) course was equivalent to a degree (Level 5 qualification), it was cheaper than a BA Hons and taught TV and film production.

After my course I got talking to the Editor-in-Chief of *Reader's Digest* magazine, as I was praising them for including a regular feature on native wildlife. She checked out some of the videos I was putting on YouTube and must have liked them as she commissioned me to make a mini-series for the magazine's website. My series acted as a seasonal guide to British fauna and flora, which I entitled *Wildlife Monthly*. For over a year and for two series, each month I researched, wrote, presented, filmed and edited three nature videos, highlighting conservation stories and what wildlife to look out for. It helped spread awareness of the natural world, thus helping conservation in some way.

In the winter after I ended my series with the magazine, there happened to be an irruption (a sudden increase in animal population) of Bohemian waxwings. A flock was seen at Webbs of Wychbold an award-winning garden centre in Worcestershire, feeding on some light pink Sorbus berries. I managed to capture some lovely footage of them and after putting a video online it caught the attention of people on Twitter and journalists at BBC *Midlands Today*. So, naturally I was interviewed again, showcasing my footage and waxing lyrical about these glam/punk-looking birds.

A couple of years ago, Jamie Wyver and I made a short video for fun to promote International Dawn Chorus Day, which a director at Cambridge TV (now called That's Cambridge) saw. We were invited down to the TV station, they wanted us to reproduce the video for them in June, but as the dawn chorus is over by then we discussed making a feature about bird song. We must have impressed them as we walked away with a commission for a TV series. The series was called *The Wild Side*, it has five episodes in which Jamie and I discovered the wildlife in and around Cambridgeshire, meeting the people who help nature thrive across the county! Dedicated volunteers, scientists, nature reserve staff and enthusiasts tell their stories and give tips on wildlife-watching and conservation.

More recently I went back to college to do a Level 3 Diploma — City & Guilds, Conservation, Countryside & The Environment. This is a practical hands-on course taught in the Birmingham Botanical Gardens at The Study Centre in which I gained experience. With visits to a variety of wildlife sites we are expected to work with the Wildlife Trust for Birmingham and the Black Country and other groups. The Birmingham Botanical Gardens has a large wildlife area (Site of Local Importance for Nature Conservation or SLINC) with woodland, a large pond and a stream where some of the practical work is carried out — studying environmental and land-based businesses, boundary habitat conservation, ecological surveys and techniques, and the improvement of British habitats. Plus, the ecology of trees/woods/forests, freshwater/wetland conservation and game management.

Also, the past two years I've been making videos at the BBC's *Gardeners' World Live Show* at the NEC, Birmingham, advocating wildlife gardening; interviewing the Editor-in-Chief of *Gardeners' World* magazine, two presenters from the show, and several show garden winners, all about the nature aspect of gardening, how important it is, and what they had done to encourage wildlife in their show gardens.

Adam L Canning is a naturalist, wildlife filmmaker and broadcaster.

9

Be open to
ADVICE

— — — — — — — — — — — — — — — —

BLOG (June): My heart was in my mouth, there were butterflies in my stomach, and my jaw had just hit the floor plus a number of other metaphors I could think of.

The producer had just told me that five of my wildlife photos were going to be critiqued by the presenter on live TV in front of a studio full of people.

Taking criticism isn't easy at the best of times. Nobody likes to be told that they could have done something better or in a different way. The words that particular presenter used as he critiqued my photos were: 'If you were to tell me that this was the best picture in the world, I would say to you, what are you going to do tomorrow? Because I think as photographers, as artists, we can all continue to improve and we will only improve if we are critical of our work, so we see what we've done wrong, so we can put it right'.

Having someone more experienced than myself who was offering to give advice, to help me improve my photography in a way that was constructive, showed me that he was willing to pass on his experience and knowledge and I was grateful for that. Even if the butterflies in my stomach were just about to explode all over the studio.

— — — — — — — — — — —

Not all advice is good advice. You need to have the confidence and self-belief to accept help, to be open to it, but also be ambitious and strong enough to do things your own way when necessary.

A Focus on Nature

A great place to start to is A Focus on Nature — a network set up for young professional and amateur nature conservationists in the UK. The aim is for all members to learn from and help each other, through meetings, get-togethers, a mentoring scheme and a youth forum. It is predominantly aimed at 16 to 30-year-olds but many younger people also get involved and are enthusiastically welcomed and supported.

When you are young, and especially in that horrendous era of puberty where each choice you make or thing you say could be a disastrous step in social quicksand, it is very easy to want to shove your life's passion for natural history away, as if it were dirty clothes under the bed. To become a false shell of who you are, pretending to like the bands and sports you know nothing of, with the disguise you try to create putting you at unease and therefore at odds with others. Don't do this. I know because it's what I did.

Confidence, knowledge and passion are weapons in their own right. Put together they are unstoppable. Break past the inevitable jeers as people realise how different you are, and suddenly it will turn into respect.

Peter Cooper — A Focus on Nature

Recommended
READING

Non-fiction

Badger Behaviour, Conservation and Rehabilitation: 70 Years of Getting to Know Badgers — George E Pearce.

Badgered to Death: The People and Politics of the Badger Cull — Dominic Dyer

Badgerlands: The Twilight World of Britain's Most Enigmatic Animal — Patrick Barkham.

The Beauty in the Beast: Britain's Favourite Creatures and the People Who Love Them — Hugh Warwick.

Beyond the Beach: The Secret Wild Swims of Torbay — Matt Newbury and Sophie Pierce.

Birdwatching With Your Eyes Closed: An Introduction to Birdsong — Simon Barnes.

British Wildlife Photography Awards — Various volumes.

Collins Bird Guide: The Most Complete Guide to the Birds of Britain and Europe — Lars Svensson, Killian Mullarney, Dan Zetterström, Peter J Grant.

The Great British Year: Wildlife Through the Seasons — Stephen Moss.

Halcyon River Diaries — Philippa Forrester and Charlie Hamilton James.

Hunting the Hunted: At War with the Whalers — Laurens de Groot.

The Inner Life of Animals: Surprising Observations of a Hidden World — Peter Wohlleben.

The Nature Tracker's Handbook (RSPB) — Nick Baker.

100 Ways to Take Better Nature and Wildlife Photographs — Guy Edwardes.

100 Things that Caught My Eye — Chris Packham.

Photographing Wildlife in the UK: Where and How to Take Great Wildlife Photographs — Andrew Marshall.

Pocket Guide to the Butterflies of Great Britain and Ireland — Richard Lewington.

RSPB Spotlight Series — Various authors: books on a variety of individual animals.

Steve Backshall's Wildlife Adventurer's Guide: A Guide to Exploring Wildlife in Britain — Steve Backshall.

Watching Waterbirds: 100 Birds … in Just One Day! — Kate Humble and Martin McGill.

Fiction

Animals of Farthing Wood — Colin Dann.

The Last Wild — Piers Torday.

My Name is Mina — David Almond.

The Queen of Speckled Wood — S W Teal.

The River Singers — Tom Moorhouse.

The Wolf Wilder — Katherine Rundell.

Magazines

Amateur Photographer.

BBC Wildlife Magazine.

How it Works.

Outdoor Photography.

Websites

- afocusonnature.org — The Youth Nature Network. A place where young naturalists can network, find a mentor and join in with events.
- badgerland.co.uk — Guide to all things badgers.
- bbc.com/earth/uk — Photos and film clips on nature from around the world.
- discoverwildlife.com — BBC Wildlife magazine website that runs alongside the printed edition.
- first-nature.com — Fantastic website for identifying anything from birds, to insects, trees and fungi.
- garden-birds.co.uk — Lots of details on British birds.
- mammal.org.uk — Information about mammals, training, latest research and events.
- rspb.org.uk — Help with bird identification, list of reserves to visit, latest campaigns and a kids area.
- wildlifekate.co.uk — Brilliant website with live webcams and footage of the Yew View garden.
- wildlifetrusts.org — UK nature reserves, events, competitions and volunteering in your area.

ACKNOWLEDGEMENTS

I would like to thank my publisher, Alex Gibson. Not many publishers will even consider looking at work from a teenager.

Special thanks go to my amazing family, particularly my mum, who in her words acts as my 'unpaid PA', and my sister for, well, putting up with me.

This book would not have been possible without all those who contributed to it, not only because they did, but also because as each quote, contribution, hint or phrase came in it encouraged me to carry on. I admire each and every one of you.

At the beginning, it was BBC *Wildlife Magazine* staff members Ben Hoare, Matt Swaine and Jo Price who believed in me enough to take me on as a Local Patch Reporter when I was just ten-years-old.

In addition, I would like to single out Ben Garrod who has helped me more than he can possibly imagine and Chris Packham for all his support too.

I am extremely grateful to my local farmer, David Gow, as without his permission I wouldn't have been able to have access to photograph and interact with my local wildlife.

One last mention goes to Oxford Badger Group, especially Emily Lawrence, my second unofficial PA(!), Barbara Witkowski, Julia and Linda. Oxford's badgers are lucky to have such a dedicated group.

Stay Wild

Alex

INDEX